Summerson Shenanigans

A memoir of growing up in the 1950s and 60s

by

Denise Jones

Copyright © 2020 Denise Jones
All rights reserved
ISBN: 979-8-5547-6307-6.

Dedication

Dedicated to Kitty Knibb.
My sister-in-law and pal.
I so miss our chats and laughs together, Kit.
Hope you and Ronnie are not causing
too much chaos up there.
God bless!

Acknowledgements

Thanks to my great bunch of friends at Formby writers for their ongoing support, help and motivation.

To the Facebook groups of *'Newquay Nostalgia'* and *'You know you grew up in Newquay when you remember........'*, who have been a constant fountain of information, especially old school pals.

To my 'Techno Babes' WhatsApp group (you know who you are!) who have been on at me for years to get this book finished.

Lastly, to my sister Frances, with whom, I have spent many a happy hour debating and challenging our recollections of past events, looking through photos and sharing some lovely memories together.

Chapter list

	Page
The Grocer's shop	1
London Life	9
Are we there yet?	21
Cornwall here we come	27
White Sails, Holywell Bay	39
Our Holy Well	52
Blue Lagoon take 1	64
Mind your grammar	70
Growing up	82
Don't tell the guests	93
Cornish v Cockney	104
Pass the sick bucket	113
Sand, sea and surfers	121
Blue Lagoon take 2	132
Mind the stairs	142
Chatty chambermaids	155
Christmas cry-baby	165
Careful what you wish for	175
Party time	182
Treninnick Tavern	191
All night long	203
All creatures, great and small	215
The 'goings on'	224
Liverpool here I come	231
The Bust up	239
Epilogue - Into the frying pan	250

	Page
Glossary & Info	253
Map of Newquay	255
List of Newquay Hotels & Owners	256
Newquay Shops	257
Author bio	261

Photographs

Page

Cover	Me in garden at White Sails.
xvi	Trenance Gardens.
xvi	Great Western beach towards harbour.
xvi	Huer's Hut.
1	Me in pram outside Grocer's shop.
4	Grocer's shop, 807 Harrow Rd Willesden.
9	193 Wembley Hill road.
10	Me and Mum in garden at Wembley.
14	Frances, me and Cliff in London.
18	Jubbly Orange drink.
19	Tom & Anne Cull left, Mum & Dad right Easter 1935.
28	Our caravan on Trenance camp site.
29	Frances, Dad, Cliff and me on Harbour
30	White Sails, centre, with battlements
31	Treguth Inn, Holywell Bay.
34	Linda, Chum and me.
36	Cubert school. C 2014
40	Linda Gray & me outside Holywell cafe
42	Me in front garden at White Sails.
44	Mum, me with Linda in foreground.
45	Me, Linda and friend on Holywell Beach.
46	Monkey rock on Holywell beach.
53	Uncle Frank right, Sandra left and Frances inside the Holy Well.
61	Nicky Mitchell, far left, Cliff 3rd from right, Frances, far right, me front, Holywell

Page

62	Gull rocks, Holywell Bay beach.
63	Me at Cubert school aged 11.
70	Newquay Grammar school. c 2014
72	Dad in tea hut in White Sails garden.
73	White Sails tearoom tables & umbrellas.
77	Newquay Harbour.
90	Our family at top of Harbour.
97	Treninnick House.
100	Trevithick House.
105	Frances and Alan's wedding.
114	Mrs Tamblyn, left, Leslie Mather front, me centre, Charmaine right, courtesy of Western Morning News.
116	Me, Charmaine Stoneman & Jenny Critchley on cruise ship.
119	Classmates on cruise. L to R – Charmaine, Jenny, Steve Hall. Adrian Johns, Paul Cooke?, Rafe Critchley, Leslie Mather & Paul Ashmore sitting
123	The Slope down to Great Western Beach.
126	View across Great Western.
128	Ferry to France. Dad, Cliff, Me, Peter Phillips, Mum, Jack & Connie Phillips, Alan Greenland.
134	Old photo of Blue Lagoon.
144	Minerva hotel. C 2014
157	Viaduct in Newquay.
159	Killacourt, towards Atlantic hotel.
167	Hotel Bristol. C 2016
169	Bristol chambermaids. Liverpool Barbara, Me, Irish Cathy, Barbara ?, Irish Mary.

184	Bristol chambermaids getting ready for night out. Barbara ?, Liverpool Margaret, Me at back Liverpool Barbara and Charmaine.
185	Chris Jones at Sailors fancy dress 1968, Charmaine & Pinky Tippett in background.
187	Pat's mates from Liverpool at Tall Trees, Jimmy Johnson, Tony Farrell, John Clark, Frank Coulson, Joey Disley.
188	Victoria Hotel staff, Terry lewis, far left, Margaret Lewis, sitting front. Josie Cobley behind her, Tony Cobley 4th from right back, Pat, 5th right at back.
189	Beachcroft Hotel beer mat
192	Treninnick House
195	Me behind bar, Treninnick
196	Me, Mum and Dad behind Treninnick bar
198	Postcards and keyring giveaways
199	Mum, Alan & Frances, New Year's Eve fancy dress
201	The Tavern, Dad, Mum, Connie Phillips, me, Ann's friend, Ann Jones, Jack Phillips, Chris and Cliff
208	Old photo of Central Hotel
210	Millbay laundry basket
212	Pat at rear of Fore street bedsit
212	Pat on moped, Fore street
220	The Central Inn c 2014
234	Me on the Ferry across the Mersey 1969
237	Top- Saturday night in Liverpool, Carol Lunt, Kitty Knibb, Lily Traynor and me right 1971
237	Bottom- Jerry Garrity, Ronnie Knibb, Pat and Tommy Traynor 1969
238	Pat, Lily & Ann (Pat's sisters), me, Pat's Mum 1969

238	Jerry Garrity, Ronnie Knibb, Tommy Traynor, ?, Pat and Pat's Mum
240	Wedding group photo, Tower Rd church
240	My wedding day, back garden at Treninnick. Dad, Mum, Chris, Me, Frances, Alan, Cliff, Mandy and Luci in front.
241	Wedding evening. Me and Pat
242	Mum doing the twist with Alan
243	Pat, Brian Dirkin, Jackie Perkins and Frank Jones.
248	Pat, Paul and his Dad outside the cottage

Author's note

I believe everything in this book to be correct. However, as my memory isn't as good as it was, I have sometimes relied on others for information.

Therefore, if I have documented any names, dates, places or events incorrectly, then I sincerely apologise.

Or, if I have upset anyone by misrepresenting the facts, can I assure you, it was not my intention to offend.

If, after reading this book, you would like to clarify or comment on anything, then please message me, via Facebook.

Or, if you would like to leave a review, good or otherwise, please do, via Amazon.

Any helpful feedback would be much appreciated.

Introduction

My parent's lust for life, imagination and *have a go* mentality certainly made for a colourful childhood for us kids. Even when we lived in London's suburbia, Mum and Dad constantly sought new opportunities and with their hobbies, interesting ventures and our weekends spent visiting the many relatives scattered all over the city, our lives were never dull.

So, it was no real surprise, in 1955, when I was four, while we still lived in Wembley, they also bought a dilapidated house called White Sails in Holywell Bay, North Cornwall and well, that was a different ball game altogether. The beach became my new back garden and the rolling sand dunes my playground. The sand so scorching hot, it burnt your feet if you forgot your plastic beach shoes.

I was free to explore, splash around in the crystal-clear stream leading down to the Atlantic Ocean or learn to surf on my short wooden surfboard.

No more busy roads to cross, no more hustle and bustle, no more noise and pollution, no more smog. Just the peace and tranquillity of a Cornish village, for a few months of the year anyway, because mine was an unconventional childhood.

We would spend all the winter months in London and then come April, we'd load up the car and drive to Cornwall, spending the glorious summers down there and then do the reverse trip back to London every October. This lasted for five years, before we eventually moved down to Cornwall full time in 1960.

Dad had slowly turned White Sails into self-contained holiday flats, and we were fully initiated into the frantic world of 'The Summer season'. Then, when I was twelve, we moved into Newquay and I was happily thrust into an even more wonderfully exciting, cosmopolitan frenzy.

The town heaved during the Summer months from Easter until October when the doors of every hotel, guest house and Bed and Breakfast swung open and welcomed the never-ending stream of holiday makers. Families of all ages and backgrounds. Beaches were packed, pasties and Cornish cream teas the foods of choice and Scrumpy cider the source of many a drunken night.

Of course, it was in the Sixties when surfing really took off and where local talented surfers rubbed shoulders with Aussie lifeguards, resplendent in fluorescent Bermuda shorts carrying Malibu boards, exposing bronzed bodies. There was a lot to like!

For the locals, which we now were, lives were choreographed around summer. Planning for it, talking about it, living it. If your family didn't make enough money during the Summer season to see you through the long quiet winter, when everything shut down, you wouldn't survive.

Maximising every bit of space was essential. You couldn't be precious about giving up your bedroom for paying guests. While the rest of the country made plans to go on their summer holidays, we *were* their summer holidays. Everyone worked non-stop to make sure you enjoyed your time by the seaside, whether you came from the Ford's three week shut down or Scotland's two-week break, hired a caravan or stayed in a luxury hotel.

Those holidaymakers had to be catered for, so staff were employed from all over the country, lured by the promise of working in a fabulous location, getting three meals a day, and living accommodation. There were Scousers, Brummies, Londoners, they came from everywhere, all escaping from the shackles of city life or freedom from family or just to have a job and learn to surf and walk around in flip flops for most of the day.

These different factions of locals, surfers, holidaymakers, and hotel workers usually rubbed along nicely, but every so often they collided head on. As a naïve and shy sixteen-year old fresh out of school, I struggled to fit in with the brashness and confidence of those city slicker hotel workers, but working as a chambermaid, waitress, barmaid then hotel receptionist, I slowly got an education that school could never provide and what an education *that* turned out to be!

So, if you've ever worked in the Tourist Industry, you will appreciate and empathise with the stories I tell and the sheer pandemonium that can go on behind the scenes. If, however, you've never had the privilege of working a summer season, then be prepared for an adventurous romp as I escort you through escapades that will make you laugh, shed a few tears, possibly give you panic attacks or just make you cringe.

But I begin my story in London and explain what my life was like, as a child, living in the Capital in the early 1950s. How our move to Cornwall came about. How living in Holywell Bay was magical and how, as a teenager in the 1960s, Newquay was just the most fantastic place to be.

The Grocer's shop

'Come on love, open the door, there's a dear, turn the key to the left.'

It was the early 1950s and Mum and Dad had a greengrocer's shop on the high street at 807 Harrow road, in Willesden, North London. They'd lived above the shop before I was born, with my older sister Frances and elder brother Clifford. But when I came along in 1951 that became too small for us all, so they bought a house in Wembley. With my siblings being at school and no-one else to look after me at home, they'd take me with them to the shop every day.

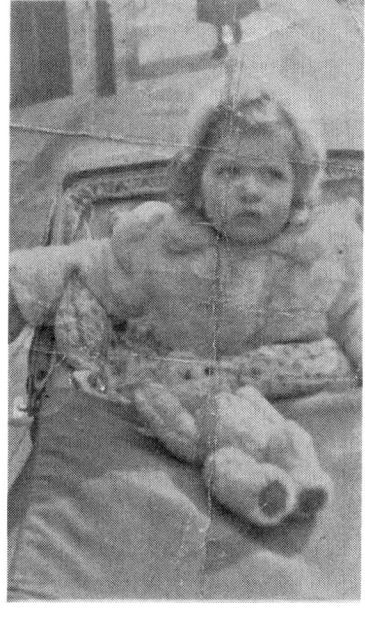

As a baby, they'd park me outside in my huge Silver cross pram, out of harm's way, or at least out of their way. It seems that I was the entertainment for the regular customers, who would tickle me under the chin, make funny faces at me or throw a coochy-coo in my direction as they went into the shop, ration book in hand.

I remember sitting outside in that pram or like to think I do, but perhaps it's just my mum telling me about it that I remember. When I was walking and a bit older, I was much more troublesome, constantly getting under their feet, desperate to explore.

On one such 'expedition' I'd slipped away, up the back stairs to the next floor, to go to the lavatory as we called it then. I could go on my own, but it was a bit of an effort to sit on the seat as my little legs were too short to reach the floor so dangled over the edge. Dad had attached a piece of string to the chain, but I still had to stand on tip toes to flush it and when I did, the pipes rattled, the cistern wobbled, erupting into such a loud explosive gurgle, that I'd rush for the door. Only this time I couldn't get out. I'd locked myself in.

It was ages before they noticed I was missing.

'Stop crying now dear, we'll soon have you out, just turn the key to the left,' Mum said again soothingly, trying to cajole me into action, but I knew I'd be in big trouble. I'd been told never to lock the door and how I'd managed to turn the long brown heavy key, I don't know. Now sobbing uncontrollably, it was not the best time trying to teach me my left from my right!

Sitting shivering on the freezing lino floor, head buried into my knees pulled up to my chest, I heard Dad's voice.

'Come on now big ears, what's all this?'

I looked up to see him struggling to get in the window, which Mum had luckily left open after cleaning up that morning. He'd borrowed the ladder from the window cleaner next door and despite his gangly thin and lanky build, it took him a few attempts to clamber in through the narrow metal frame. His bony ribs clearly visible, straining against his shirt. Knocking the tin of Vim scouring powder, Mum had left on the window ledge, sending it shooting across the floor leaving a trail of white powder in its wake.

'Okay Bacon Bonce,' I snivelled through my snotty tears, as he scooped me up, with his big working man's hands, wiping my eyes with his hanky before unlocking the door.

When he was serving in the shop, Dad always wore a long white apron which he tied around his neck and waist. I'd watch him carve the huge piece of gammon ham that Mum had boiled in the small kitchen out the back or cut a slab of cheese off the big block with the lethal looking wire cutter. Then weigh everything out carefully on the triangular shaped Avery scales. There was no such thing as self-service. The till was just a wooden drawer underneath the counter, no fancy push button affair for Dad. He'd add up a person's bill mentally as he went along.

The high glass counter to the right had shelves behind on the back wall, with tins of Spam, Libby's fruit medley, Heinz salad cream, Bisto gravy and Camp coffee, Carnation milk, tins of pink salmon, Bird's custard, Lyons tea, and small jars of fish paste. I loved Spam fritters and Mum's favourite was tinned fruit especially mandarin segments and evaporated milk, or 'evap' as she called it, a regular treat after our tea.

There were eggs stamped with a little lion on them, water biscuits and Wright's coal tar soap next to the tins of Ajax and Vim. Below those shelves against the back wall were big square biscuit tins that had half glass lids and were tilted so customers could see the biscuits inside, such as Nice, Bourbon, Ginger nuts and Shortcake. With rationing still in place for a lot of items, the tin of cheaper broken biscuits was a popular crowd-pleaser.

Sugar, butter, cheese, margarine, cooking fat, bacon, meat and tea were all still rationed, with sugar rationing not ending until 1953 and meat rationing in 1954. Cliff and Frances used to get pocket money by helping Dad fill small blue waxed bags with currants, sultanas, rice, or sugar, from the big brown sacks in the storeroom behind the shop. These small bags would sit on the shelf opposite the front door and as their treat, for helping, Dad would give them each a penny to buy a miniature Hovis loaf, from the bakery down the street.

In the kitchen out back, Mum also made individual meat pies to sell in the shop in small enamel dishes with the blue rim, which were so popular, they sold in a flash. The window display consisted of tins, tins and more tins, piled high, neat and symmetrical. They didn't sell any fresh fruit and veg, because most people grew their own or bought from street markets, or were given by neighbours, who had surplus.

Mum and Dad hadn't always been greengrocers though. My parents, Alfred George and Doris Rose Bullen came from typical east end London families, Dad from Walthamstow and Mum from Hackney , the grittier side of London.

Where it was the norm for newly married couples to set up home in the front room of relatives' terraced houses. Where you had an outside loo, a tin bath in front of the fire and you left school at thirteen or fourteen with no formal qualifications.

Dad was an engineer by trade, having completed his apprenticeship, but he could turn his hand to anything, building, plumbing, carpentry, car mechanic, you name it. Mum had been trained by a Jewish tailor as a seamstress and she made all our clothes and soft furnishings, kept house, worked in the shop and cooked lovely home-made meals.

Her rice pudding, made with creamy and sweet condensed milk, had a thick layer of nutmeg on the top and crispy bits around the outside of the tin dish, that us siblings always fought over. It was my all-time favourite.

She knitted all our sweaters, and I could plain and pearl with the best of them, by the time I was six. Can't remember ever having shop bought clothes as a child as hand me downs from my sister were mandatory. Make do and mend the order of the day. I loved the coloured smocking though, she did on many of my little dresses.

She had it hard growing up. Her parents separated when she was a youngster and when she married Dad in 1937, her own Mum was gravely ill in hospital, so after the wedding ceremony they visited her, so she could see my Mum in her wedding dress. My Grandmother died a few weeks later.

Dad tried many new ventures over the years, veering away from engineering for a while in the late 1930s, starting a removal firm, with just one huge van that had Bullen's removals emblazoned on the side. Mum often went with him on the long trips up and down the country before they had us kids and they visited many different places, which I think sowed the seed for their desire to eventually move away from London.

But then World War 2 broke out.

Dad's skills as an engineer were thought to be too valuable, for him to go away to war. Therefore, his contribution was to manage an ammunitions factory, where Mum also worked on the production line.

It was imperative that they kept the troops supplied with ammunition, so their stories of how they kept churning it out twenty-four seven, despite bombs dropping all around them, were chilling. London was devastated by the bombing, which was still evident in the early 1950s, when I remember seeing bombed out sites still around the city, on our Sunday car trips out.

After the war, while rationing was still in place, Dad seized the opportunity and that's when he opened the Greengrocers shop. When rationing finally stopped in 1954, some nine years after the end of the war, the greengrocery business had suddenly lost its appeal for him and when his application to turn the shop into a launderette was refused, he sold it and temporarily went back to engineering.

At home in Wembley, Dad was forever mending or building something, so I rarely saw him out of his petrol blue overalls, which only seemed to emphasise how thin he was.

His thick coarse wavy dark brown hair that I inherited was never free of dust or wood chippings and his big workman's hands got slathered with Swarfega to rid them of dirt and grease at the end of the day.

Then there was the pencil permanently stuck behind his ear, handy for jotting down any measurements or marking a plank of wood ready to be sawn. His love of Fishermen's Friend lozenges was soon passed down to me and their unmistakeable strong fiery heat was the go-to for curing a cough or sore throat, but I just loved the taste.

I'll always treasure those early years in the shop, because of my visits to Mrs Moore, who lived in the top floor flat. Whenever I was allowed, I'd climb the stairs and knock on her door.

She always had a bowl of cold boiled potatoes on her kitchen table and she would let me take one as my treat. To this day I always boil a few extra potatoes and when I have them cold the next day with loads of salt and pepper, I think of her.

My sister tells me that in 1953, Dad bought Mrs Moore a small black and white television set to watch the Queen's coronation as a thank you for looking after my sister and me whilst Mum and Dad camped out with my brother to watch the Queen's coronation procession pass by.

I often think of Mrs Moore and those early carefree years, when it was safe to leave me in that pram outside!

London Life

'Muuuummm, Denise is having another nosebleed, come quick'

Whenever that cry went up, Mum would rush me upstairs to Olive, our lodger who was a nurse. She rented the large room at the top of the stairs, of the four-bedroomed semi-detached, where we lived at 193 Wembley Hill road, Wembley. I hardly ever saw her, except when I had those very heavy, scary nose bleeds. She had her own front door key, own cooker and sink in her room, so came and went as she pleased, without disturbing anyone.

I shared a bedroom with my sister Frances at the

back overlooking the garden. Our brother Cliff had the small box room at the front, with Mum and Dad in the other large bedroom next to him. We had an indoor bathroom, a garage for Dad's beloved car and a long back garden. Dad was passionate about gardening and the tall canes for tethering his runner beans were a regular sight in the vegetable patch at the bottom.

Mum would have to scrub the mud and soil from the lettuce, potatoes, onions, or carrots or whatever we were having for our tea before they appeared on our dinner plate. Caterpillars found in the lettuce were a regular occurrence as was finding a worm wriggling in an apple picked from the large tree which shaded half the garden.

Those nose bleeds were just one of the challenges I faced growing up. I seemed to do a lot of crying back then. Mum took us kids to get our photos taken one Christmas and there isn't one good one of me, when I'm not snivelling or scowling.

I had wild curly unmanageable thick hair, like Dad, that Mum struggled to get a comb through. I inherited long thin feet and bad eyesight

from Auntie Betty, Dad's younger sister and Mum dragged me to the Doctor because I was so very thin with arms like matchsticks.

But when he found out I was eating well, with plenty of Dad's home-grown vegetables and a cod liver oil capsule every day, he told her there was nothing to worry about. Cod liver oil had been recommended for children to take after the war and Mum had an enormous brown jar sitting right by the kitchen table, so she wouldn't forget to give us each one after our tea. They were so large, I had trouble swallowing before the foul-tasting liquid would ooze out into my mouth. I'd pull a face and grimace, but she wouldn't leave my side, until I'd proved to her I'd swallowed it, by sticking my tongue out.

If I had a chill, which was quite often, Mum would warm a large piece of lint on the Esse hotplate cover and then lather it in camphorated oil and apply to my chest under my nightdress, to help me breathe easier at night.

My bad eyesight materialised when my teacher realised that I couldn't read the blackboard. Mum took me to the opticians who told her that I should only need them for distance. Just as well, as I hated wearing the small round glasses with wiry arms that curled around my ears like limpets.

But if all that wasn't enough, there was my painful shyness, I had to contend with. Something I have struggled with all my life. A proper scaredy cat sometimes, when strangers visited the house, like the coal man who terrified the life out of me. The whites of his eyes peering out at me, being the only part of him not covered in thick black coal dust as he carried the heavy sacks on his shoulder to the coal shed. I'd cling on to Mum's skirt and bury my head in her apron, afraid to look at him.

Then there was my first encounter with boys, aged six. I was sitting cross legged on the polished wooden floor, in the queue outside the school canteen one day, waiting to be allowed in for my school dinner, when suddenly a boy in front slid a small box of chocolates over to me.

I felt myself go red, so embarrassed. I didn't know what to do, so hid them in the sliding cupboard above my bed headboard. My sister Frances spilled the beans to Mum, one night when we were getting our Sunday night bath. We all got in the same bath water once a week, with my brother being the last as he was always the grubbiest.

Frances and I would play Jacks or Straws on the hall lino floor or she and Cliff would take me to the park to play. I loved the roundabout and the slides best, but one day Cliff was pushing me on the swing, when I suddenly let go and flew into mid-air, landing on the harsh gravel.

I screamed all the way home as they manhandled me between them, struggling to carry me, as I sobbed uncontrollably. It wasn't until I got a cuddle from Mum and she gently bathed my grazes, did my snivelling stop. The distinct yellowish brown of the soothing iodine which she'd plastered on my knees took days to fade.

What I really loved to do though, was to dress up and dance. Mum and Dad would be watching the Billy

Cotton Band Show which started on television in 1957 on our black and white set, while I'd be prancing around behind the settee.

'Wakey, Wakey,' Billy would shout at the beginning of each programme as I'd be trying to copy the dancers in their feathers and glittery costumes. But if Mum turned around to watch me, I'd stop, shouting at her to turn back. So, she packed me off to tap dance classes with Frances and at Christmas, they put on a show. I had a costume that Mum had made, stockings and those proper white tap shoes with ribbons at the front that you tied. Being one of the little ones they put me right at the front and after only a few minutes tapping away, my stockings gave up trying to defy gravity on my skinny legs and started sliding down.

I carried on tapping away as they lodged themselves firmly around my ankles which highly amused the audience and their laughter resulted in me collapsing into a flood of tears, again. I was rescued only by my sister taking my hand and leading me off the stage as I was blubbering.

The Esse range cooker that kept the kitchen lovely and warm was where Mum would often pull up Dad's tall wing back wooden chair right next to, when he was at work. The sky-blue painted chair with the floral cushion that Mum had made, where he'd sit of an evening and let me climb on his knee for a cuddle

She'd get the best of the heat whilst she knitted, needles clicking as she listened to Mrs Dales Diary.

There would be a pan of something bubbling gently on the top hob or cooking slowly in the oven that filled the house with tempting smells.

She'd make cheese pie from the dry hard cheese bits from Dad's shop that couldn't be sold. She'd let me run my finger around the cake bowl after she'd made the mix for her Victoria sponge and her rabbit pie was a regular on the menu.

One day when we were all having our tea around the huge table in the kitchen, there was a knock at the front door. As Dad went to open it, Mum put his dinner in the bottom oven to keep warm. When he returned to enjoy the rest of his steak and kidney pudding, the horrible gunge from the melted faux ivory handles of his knife and fork that she'd forgotten to remove, had spread over his plate.

He picked up the plate and threw it against the wall, meat, gravy, peas, and potatoes splattering everywhere. It was rare for Dad to ever get angry. He was usually such a mild-mannered man.

He loved his food, my Dad. There was the bread and dripping from a Sunday roast when the fat from the cooked joint had gone hard in the dish, he'd scrape it off and have on a slab of thickly cut bread for his tea. Then there were the winkles he'd bring home that you had to prize out of their shell with a pin and not forgetting our visits to the famous tiled interiors of the pie and mash shops down Walthamstow market. He'd relish the pie and mash that he had to eat with a spoon as it was swimming in lashings of that famous green liquor, which in more modern times I believe is a parsley gravy.

Milk would be delivered by the milkman, no supermarkets back then. You had all separate shops for your meat and fish and groceries and bread, with bread and meat being wrapped in tissue paper.

Mum would go mad every morning when she brought in the bottles of milk from the doorstep and the tops had been pecked out by the birds, who had siphoned up the thick cream.

We had a piano in the front room, where Cliff had his piano lessons, having to practise the same piece of music, 'Fur Elise' over and over. It was *so* boring. Even worse was the metronome that sat on the top of the piano, which was supposed to help him keep in time. It became hypnotic if you watched it for too long. He wasn't a natural piano player, like Dad, but he did try, bless him.

He would rather have been messing about with his Meccano set in his tiny bedroom or making a plane to hang from the ceiling from an Air Fix kit someone had bought him for his birthday. He loved stamp collecting and would pester anyone going away, to send a postcard, just so he could steam off the stamp and stick it in his album.

In summer, Mum sometimes took me to the open-air swimming pool nearby or make a makeshift tent in the garden by hanging blankets over the washing line, by the doors leading out from the living room. In Winter we'd occasionally go to the Ice show at Wembley Arena.

The pony and cart of the rag and bone man could regularly be heard clip clopping down our road.

'Any old iron,' he'd shout, although you could hardly make out what he said, especially if it was muffled by the dreaded smog. The thick wall of yellowish pollution would greet us regularly in the Winter when we opened our front door and the cloying chemical smell so strong, we'd be told to pull our scarves over our faces, so as to not to breathe it in and damage our lungs. A pea souper, Dad called it.

After they sold the shop, Mum didn't go out to work, but her skills as a seamstress were always in demand. Most evenings there would be strangers knocking and filing into the front room for fittings for a frock or suit or such like. Her beloved Singer treadle sewing machine had pride of place in the corner and was rarely still. I'd sit on the stairs and peek through the banisters to get a closer look, but she'd usually close the door over, much to my annoyance.

The one thing I hated about that house was the quiet in the afternoons if I wasn't at school. Mum always had to have her afternoon nap which she carried on throughout her life. She only needed about an hour and then she'd get up, make a cup of tea, come to and be ready for the rest of the day. All I can remember is the relentless tick tock of the clock on the mantelpiece, whilst I sat fidgeting, bored out of my mind, with her keep telling me to *'sit still.'* She always carried smelling salts in her handbag, and I would regularly see her take a sniff, especially if she needed a bit of a boost after her nap.

Being only a stone's throw away from Wembley stadium, on Cup final day, my siblings would hold my hands tight and we'd stand outside our house, waiting for the winning supporters who'd throw coins to us, from their passing coaches.

Mum and Dad would be glued to the black and white television watching Cliff Mitchelmore on the new Tonight programme which started in 1957 and I'd hide behind the settee, too afraid to watch Quatermass, a scary sci fi thriller which aired the following year.

My favourite television was Rag, Tag and Bobtail, the Wooden tops and Bill and Ben and I remember sitting with Mum after lunch waiting for 'Listen with Mother' to come on the radio. It was a lady telling a story, but before she started to read would say…

'Are you sitting comfortably, …then I'll begin.' Mum would sometimes take me into the sweet shop on

the corner on the way home from school. Occasionally, she'd buy me a 'Jubbly' a frozen orange drink in a large triangular shaped carton, which is, I believe, the inspiration behind Del Boys' saying 'Lovely Jubbly' in Only Fools and Horses. If you cut the corner off, you could suck it like a lolly, and it would last for hours.

The sweets were in jars on shelves all around the shop and you could buy two ounces or a quarter and they'd be put in a paper bag, or four for a penny, such as fruit salads or blackjacks or sherbet lemons. Sweet cigarettes with red ends, penny pipes or huge wagon wheels were my favourites though, costing a little more. This was the same shop where we returned our lemonade bottles and got a two-pence refund for every bottle.

As a treat, Dad would sometimes bring home a small blocks of ice cream and a bottle of cream soda to make ice cream sodas that would fizz and bubble and you'd end up with the delicious froth all around your mouth if you drank it too quick. There would always be a little bit of ice-cream at the bottom of the glass to be scooped out and savoured.

It was in Wembley, I learned to play cards. Although we had a television, playing cards was something we did in the evenings when we had visitors, such as Mum's sister, my Auntie Lena and Uncle Frank. Proper cockneys, Auntie Lena had such a wicked laugh, I couldn't help but laugh along with her, even if I didn't understand the joke. I learnt Rummy and Poker, Brag and Pontoon, but Canasta was my favourite. Dad and Cliff played Cribbage, but I never got the hang of that.

I loved card games so much that when we went visiting, I took a pack of cards with me, so that if I got bored with the grown-ups talking, I'd sit on the floor and play Patience. Mum loved Whist and over the years went to many a 'Whist drive'.

She also had a passion for rug making and the kits would arrive regularly. I'd be fascinated as she pulled the pre-cut pieces of wool through the canvas with the scary looking latch hook. Dad loved painting by numbers and our hall was always adorned with his latest 'artwork'.

Not sure how they packed everything into their lives, they were always doing something or going somewhere.

Dad had loads of relatives across London, but he was particularly close to Tom and Alf Cull, his cousins, who were more like brothers to him. Mum met Anne, who became her best friend when they both worked for Gumprights, Jewish tailors of Clapton Square in Hackney, in the 1930s, where they were taught all the skills of the dressmaking business. Making and mending top quality clothes ranging from the overalls which the "Nippies" used to wear, as the waitresses were called in Lyons Corner Houses, to monogrammed silk knickers for film stars or luxurious evening dresses for the wealthy upper classes.

Mum and Anne met my Dad and his cousin Tom on a night out and the four of them became inseparable, even after the two couples married in 1937. Tom and Anne moved houses quite a few times across London over the years, but we visited them throughout my childhood, no matter where they lived.

Likewise, Alf, Tom's brother and his wife Kath who lived in Walthamstow, not far from Walthamstow market and the famous Dog track, near Aunty Betty, one of Dad's sisters. I loved going to their house. Uncle Alf was always such a jolly chap, making us so welcome and they too loved playing card games. I always called my elders Aunt and Uncle, apart from my parents of course, even if they weren't, it was just a mark of respect.

Therefore, it was no surprise, that my first experience in a hotel, was a get together of Dad's relatives in Folkestone one Christmas when I was four.

What a memorable journey that turned out to be!

Are we there yet?

'You should have said no, Clifford,' my Mother raged as she twisted round from the front seat and thrust the brown paper bag into my brother's trembling hands.

Her furious stare said it all. He'd been so excited earlier that morning. Her shout of *'Don't be late,'* as he skipped out of the house to deliver his last paper round, before we set off for our Christmas holiday, had obviously gone unheeded.

'PLEEEASE can we go now,' I whined. I was so excited and couldn't wait to start this adventure. *'What is a hotel?'* I'd been asking all week.

Dad slammed the front door, gingerly negotiated the icy path, and joined the rest of us who'd been waiting in the freezing car for ages. The leather seats were so cold and slippery, I couldn't help fidgeting and kicking my sister in the process who in return kept giving me sly little digs.

'Frances, share the blanket with your sister, wrap it around her legs,' Mum said. Reluctantly my older sister did as she was told, scrunching it roughly around me, trussing me up like a chicken, tucking my little arms in so I couldn't move.

'Why do I always have to sit in the middle?' she moaned.

'You know Denise gets car sick,' Mum replied.

Dad loved driving with a passion and loved his Wolseley, with its wide running boards and 'suicide doors'. So called I came to learn, because the doors were back hinged and opened the opposite way to most car doors. With no seat belts in those days, it was very easy to fall out...or like in the American gangster movies, be pushed!

We had loads of fun days out in the car, going for picnics, visiting our multitude of relatives dispersed all over London or just finding new places to explore on our regular Sunday afternoon outings. Of course, I'd be asleep by the time we arrived home and woke up just as Dad scooped me up from the back seat and carried me up to bed, having been exhausted by all the chatter, frequent spats and arguments or singing of songs that kept us from getting bored.

We'd spend hours staring out of the windows and whenever we passed a Pub, somebody would shout, *'Fox under the Hill'* or *'Barley Mow'* or whatever it was called, so that my sister, a grown up ten, could write them down in her little book, which had letters of the alphabet listed down the side. She'd excitedly thumb through the pages to see if it had been spotted before and if not, would write the name down very slowly in her best joined up writing and whoever had spotted it, got a sweet.

Truth is, I was and still am a bad traveller in the back of a car and even though I loved those trips out, I was always so desperate to get out and stand on terra firmer. I constantly harassed my Dad by asking him when we were going to arrive at wherever it was, we were going. He never responded, just glanced at me through the rear-view mirror. I must have really got on his nerves.

The Wolseley had indicators for turning right or left that were little orange arms that shot out from the side of the car. Or Dad would just stick his arm out the open window, for turning right and sometimes ask Mum to do the same when turning left, which she was never happy about.

Sometimes, when I laid my chin on Dad's seat to get the cool breeze from his open window, I had to close my eyes to stop them from watering, he did like to drive fast. He'd rest one arm on the open window ledge, bony elbow sticking out whilst driving confidently with just the other hand and be puffing away on a mis-shapen and impossibly thin Golden Virginia and Rizla roll up, which constantly hung loosely from his mouth. Trailing tobacco falling out the end. That's how I will always remember him.

I was four and dressed in my best beige check coat, with soft chocolate brown velvet collar and cuffs that were just made to stroke. My striped woollen mittens threaded through my coat on a string because I'd lost two pairs already that winter and a bobble hat, for which I'd help make the bobbles…. well sort of. Mum had patiently tried to teach me how to do it by threading wool through the middle hole cut out in discs of cardboard, but my little fingers couldn't manage it and when it came to cut through the wool and tie the pompom, well I wasn't allowed anywhere near scissors, so that was her job.

Because Mum made all my clothes, I was well used to standing on a stool in the front room, while she pinned paper patterns on me or hemmed my dress. When those ladies came to our house to get fitted for that smart suit or cocktail dress she was making for them and Mum did forget to close the door to the front room, I'd watch with glee from the stairs when it was their turn to be tacked, pinned and twirled, to make sure the hem was level.

Christmas time was always the best though as her speciality was making costumes for local pantomime shows or kid's fancy-dress parties. The buzz of all the comings and goings of people, the vast array of vibrantly coloured ensembles hanging in the front room ready for collection; the spectacular sparkle of sequins and the drama of feathers and netting, in abundance, was thrilling.

As for knitting, well many an hour was passed where I would have to sit in front of Mum, arms outstretched as she wound balls of wool from the long skeins I had to hold, which had been freshly washed after she'd unpicked one of Dad's old sweaters or something she'd found at the local jumble sale, ready to be knitted up into something new.

'Come on now, let's all enjoy Christmas,' Dad said, eagerly trying to lighten the mood, but Mum wasn't having any of it and just stared ahead. Cliff shrank further into the far corner of the back seat, motionless and so unusually quiet, paper bag at the ready. His normally ruddy cheeks replaced by a very unnatural translucent shade of green. That day we drove in an

awkward silence, except for me frequently giggling at my brother's sorry state and pointing at him mouthing,

'You are in so…oooo much trouble.' He was my Mother's blue eye and I was enjoying the fact that he'd let her down and she was now so incredibly angry with him!

'Dad will you be playing the piano?' I asked.

'Not sure duck, the people at the hotel might not like it, so we'll have to see.'

Dad always got everybody singing at family parties, he was a great honky-tonk piano player and I loved learning 'Maybe it's because I'm a Londoner' or 'Roll out the Barrel'. I couldn't wait to play with all my cousins even if they were older than me and the repetition of getting my head patted, by all my aunts and uncles telling me how much I'd grown was something I'm sure Mum and Dad thought I'd hate. But when my relatives thrust a coin or two into my tiny hands, my shyness momentarily diminished.

'Wind down your window,' my mother eventually said to my brother, her anger obviously having abated slightly as she saw the sorry state of her eldest. He slowly wound the silver handle and stuck his head out, heavily breathing in the fresh air.

We had to stop a few times on the way to Folkestone, to dispose of the smelly sick bags. Dad finally pulled into a lay-by for our lunch stop and I eagerly jumped out onto the snow, free from the shackles of the back seat. The piping hot mug of creamy tomato soup, Mum gave us all from the big flask, steamed up my round wire rimmed spectacles. The meat paste sandwiches were cut into quarters. I had two.

'Sorry Mum,' muttered my brother sheepishly, as we all got back into the car, *'The lonely old ladies on my paper round all just wanted to have a chat and saying that one little sip of sherry wouldn't do me any harm, I couldn't hurt their feelings by saying no, could I?'*

'Well, they should have known better, you being only twelve,' she said, doing her best to stifle a smile.

We spent the rest of the journey counting all the heavy three penny pieces and shiny sixpences that they'd given him for his Christmas box and then loudly singing ten green bottles over and over.

I am sure that if my Dad were still around, his overriding memory of me would be of those long adventurous car journeys, when I would repeatedly ask him,

'Are we there yet Dad?'

Cornwall here we come

'There's the sea,' Cliff shouted.
'Where?' Frances said eagerly.
'Over there,' he said gesturing out the window.
'No, hang on....'
'There, there,' he said pointing the other way, nearly taking her eye out, as Dad drove down the steep winding road, leading to Holywell Bay. We all scrambled to get a good view between Mum and Dad's front seats. I had no chance, being the smallest. We'd turned off the A3075, Newquay to Goonhavern road, passing a sign, almost hidden by the overgrown hedge, advertising the 16th century thatched Smugglers Inn. Then on down the narrow lane, through Cubert village, past the Butchers and the Post Office on the right, with the spire, just visible, of the 14th century church opposite, set back behind stone cottages.

As the road twists and turns, the sea peeks out, then disappears. Then suddenly the dazzling deep royal blue of the Atlantic Ocean comes properly into view on the horizon, low white cottony clouds floating above. The mountainous sand dunes and steep craggy cliffs obscure the view, so the glorious Bay itself stays hidden, but I'm thrilled at seeing the place that we would eventually call home.

Mum and Dad had been holidaying in Cornwall well before I was born, camping at Liskey Hill camping site, in Perranporth, with Cliff and Frances and Mum's sister and brother-in-law Lena and Frank Heatley and their three children, my cousins, Barry, Stella, and Sandra. All crammed into Dad's removal van, with mattresses in the back for everyone to sleep on.

Dad loved it down there, so after I was born, he decided to buy a caravan from the Hoyte family on Trenance caravan site, at the bottom of Treninnick Hill in Newquay. Under the shadow of the huge rail Viaduct which transported excited holidaymakers into the town. Mum and Dad's friends Tony Richardson, who was a film director and Dana his East European wife, who lived in a large Art Deco flat in Wimbledon, also bought the neighbouring caravan.

The caravans were called Denise and Dana, which I didn't find out until recently. Dad loved driving, so the long trip down there in his beloved Wolseley car was part of his holiday, although for us kids mind-numbingly boring.

We'd play the usual game we'd made up of spotting Pub names, so my sister could write them down, but the highlight of those trips was when we stopped for something to eat in Honiton high street. We went to the same place every time. It was a sweet shop in front and a tiny café up some steps at the back and we always had fish and chips and although only visited a couple of times a year, they always remembered us and gave us a warm welcome.

For a couple of years, happy holidays were spent in the caravan, feeding the ducks, avoiding the swans or messing about in the paddle boats up and down Trenance boating lake opposite the caravan park. I can still recall the thunderous racket that the rain made on the caravan's roof.

We'd splash around in Newquay Harbour, enjoying fun family time together. Tony and Dana soon got fed up with their caravan, it wasn't really their cup of tea, so sold it to Dad and when we weren't using them, they were let out to holidaymakers.

There was a small shop on site for groceries and a toilet and shower block, so although the caravans were basic and didn't have any of today's mod cons, it was a great adventure when we stayed there. Most of the time anyway. Dad painted the caravans one year, as they were looking a bit forlorn, but nobody warned him not to paint them in the evening. When we got up the next day, the paint had all bobbled, affected by the morning dew, so they had to be painted all over again. He was not pleased.

On one such holiday Dad spotted a property for sale, called White Sails in the small village of Holywell Bay, seven miles outside Newquay, towards Perranporth.

Such a beautiful bay with magnificent golden beach and vast mountainous sand dunes.

Where your feet sank into the soft silky sand as it ran between your toes. There were rocks to climb, caves to explore and huge white surf breaking onto the near deserted beach. Dad fell in love with the quiet and seclusion of the quaint village straightaway. He was smitten. Therefore, having finally found the idyll he'd been craving, he bought it.

Just up from the bottom of the hill, on entering the village was the farmyard on the left, with the stunning 13th century, thatched Treguth Inn opposite, reputed to be haunted.

There is a small triangle of land, marking the entrance to the village and with only the one road in and out, it provides a natural roundabout, as well as a fork in the road. But it is so overgrown, you can't see through it, over it or around it, so the promise of the bay stays hidden for a while longer.

Sand covers the road, blown in from the dunes, as the left fork dips steeply down towards the St. Piran's Hotel and through security gates up to Penhale Army camp beyond. The village is higgledy-piggledy, with steep hills, mostly unmade roads and houses dotted every which way, with the only other hotel, the Holywell Bay, right at the summit, having glorious views out to sea.

You'd get to White Sails, our house, by taking the fork to the right, up the steep unmade road at the side of the café, then left along an even more potholed and rubble filled road at the back of a row of bungalows. Past the Gray's small caravan site, then the Gough's house in the dip to the left, which was just before the entrance to our house, the furthest in the village.

'It's a castle,' I said, taken aback as I spot the battlements on the roof. I didn't know what I was expecting, but I wasn't expecting that. White Sails was a wide rectangular building, standing detached on a concrete plateau, cut into the centre of a large, very steep plot of overgrown land.

It had a small extension to the right front with a bay window on the first floor above. Run-down and very unloved, its walls were crumbling and along with everything else, was in desperate need of repair, re-build and fixing, but nothing that my Dad couldn't handle, given time. A lot of time as it turned out. The 'battlements' were concrete breeze blocks painted white but made it look distinctive and different to anything I had ever seen.

But it needed loads of work to make it habitable and Dad still had to earn a living to afford to do all that was needed, so we spent all the mid to late fifties, dual living. Winters were spent in London, Dad working to save enough money so that every April, Wembley would be shut up and we'd make the long drive down to Cornwall for the whole of the summer.

With no motorways, only A roads, it was a long journey and I started with *'Are we there yet,'* as soon as we got to Staines, just outside London. But we did enjoy passing the magnificent Stonehenge and spotting the white chalk horse on the hillside. Dad would spend every waking hour, building, renovating, decorating, busily turning White Sails into self-contained holiday flats. Mum was busy making all the soft furnishings and gardening and of course still cooking us lovely meals and she was a dab hand at painting doors and skirting boards.

There was a small palm tree by the front door which turned out to be a favourite perch for long acid green crickets, whose constant chirping drove you mad. Then a concreted area immediately at the front of the house, about twenty feet wide, with a concrete wall which edged the grassed area beyond. Inlaid into the top of the wall were four flower beds which held Michaelmas daisies.

I'd be fascinated every Summer as they would open and bloom into a multitude of colour, but only when the sun came out. Then as soon as the clouds came over or it was bad weather, they'd close tight shut again. They were like our own weather barometer.

The other side of that wall was a large flat area of lawn and then the remainder of the garden dipped steeply down to the double gates at the bottom with stone steps cut into the long grass. There was no mains drainage, so there was a cesspit halfway down which would be emptied from time to time, by a huge, long pipe from a lorry parked by the gates. We all kept well out of the way when that was going on as it didn't half pong.

There were two village shops. On the left corner was Chrissie Penna's, a general store which also doubled up as the office for her caravan site which was behind her shop and bordered the path leading down to the beach. On the right was the Corner Café, which had a little general shop just inside the door and the rest was laid out for the cafe where nearly every meal on the menu included chips.

Ted and Kit Gray who owned the Corner Café, had a daughter Linda, the same age as me. As well as their older son Fred and his wife Betty and of course their dog Chum, a loveable, overgrown, soppy Collie.

Ted and Kit also had holiday flats above the café and a few caravans on a small field next to our house.

There was no love lost between the Penna and Gray families. Chrissie was Cornish, the Grays from the Midlands and both had livings to make but were in direct competition when it came to attracting holidaymakers. Us kids still had to go to school, so Frances and I were enrolled in the small school in the next village of Cubert and Cliff went to Tretherras in Newquay. My first day at Cubert school was painful. The new term had begun a few weeks earlier and I didn't know anybody. It was April 1956.

'Come now, Denise,' Mrs Dickerson, the head teacher whispered to me, as she ushered me into the small classroom. Not wanting to disturb the class too much as all the other kids were already seated and listening intently to the teacher. I was sucking my thumb and snivelling. I twisted around looking for Mum, but she'd disappeared.

The other children, sensing a slight disturbance at the back of the room, swivelled around to look at the 'new girl' as I was introduced to the class, which only made me even more upset. Mrs Race, the dark-haired teacher at the front peered over the top of her half rim glasses, smiled and gestured to a desk in the front, waited until I'd sat down and then carried on reading from Tarka the Otter.

The school only had two classrooms, not like the one in London which had hundreds of children.

Even though, at that time, when I was only there a few months of the year, I grew to like Cubert school. Well most of the time anyway.

The outside toilets at the bottom of the playground were cold and damp and had that awful slippery Izal toilet paper, that was neither use nor ornament, other than it made great tracing paper. Nigel Milward, a fellow pupil recalls getting told this by Mrs Dickerson...

'Only three sheets of toilet paper are required...one to wipe, one to make sure and one to polish.'

Thanks Nigel, I hadn't heard that gem. One time, when it was raining and I was rushing to go, the elastic on my oversized navy-blue knickers snapped and they ended up around my ankles halfway across the playground and I hated school dinners when it was sausages. Barely cooked and anaemic, they weren't like

Mum's sausages, that were all crispy and brown. I was repeatedly told off for refusing to eat them. I was still very shy but loved playing hopscotch or skipping rope or tag at playtime.

'Tag, you're it,' someone would shout, after touching your arm and you'd have to chase everyone else, to try to tag them, getting breathless and stitch in the process. I don't remember many individual names of the other children but recall families like the Carharts and Eastlakes and Trebilcocks as well as Mrs Race's son Andrew. There were a few of us pupils living in Holywell, so as buses were infrequent and we were too young to walk, our parents arranged for Pappy Wakeham to pick us up in his taxi each morning and then bring us back home again afterwards.

I didn't make a lot of friends at first, because I was only at Cubert school for a couple of months each year. From when we'd moved down from London in the April until July when the Summer holidays kicked in. Then come October, when all the holidaymakers had gone home, we'd do the reverse trip and head back up to London again for the winter and I went back to the primary school at the back of our house in Wembley.

It sounds as though we were posh having two homes, but truth be told, Mum and Dad must have bought White Sails for a pittance, the state it was in and they were always strapped for cash. Going back and forward like this went on for a few years, with each year seeing more improvements made and additional accommodation to let out to holidaymakers. Dad finally decided that White Sails was finished, so they sold the house in Wembley and we moved down to Cornwall permanently. It was April 1960. I was eight.

Frances stayed in London for a few months with her friend Lynette and her family, to finish her last few months of schooling and Cliff stayed with his pal Jimmy Foulkes and his parents, while he continued with his draughtsmanship training.

It was a time when tourism in Cornwall was the main industry and family holidays were spent in this country. Foreign holidays were not yet the 'norm' and the word 'staycation' not yet invented. We left the humdrum of nine to five suburbia behind for good and were thrust full time into this strange new world of the 'Summer Season' and all that the tourist industry entailed.

That's when our Cornish adventure really began.

White Sails, Holywell Bay

'You can take somebody's eye out throwing stones, I've a good mind to tell your parents,' the irate soldier yelled at us.

Linda Gray from the corner café and I had become great pals and we'd been sitting on the wide, open gates that led up to Penhale Army camp, her on one side and me on the other. We'd had this hair brain idea of collecting handfuls of small gravel from the roadside and as the smaller jeeps went through, throw it over the top like confetti. We giggled away enjoying this new game until this very angry soldier stopped and shouted at us. We never did that again.

Those times when the Army came to the village were brilliant. Their camp, up the other side of the hill towards Perranporth, was used now and again for training. Nobody was pre-warned when the soldiers would be on manoeuvres, so the first anybody knew was when the seemingly endless convoy of khaki lorries and jeeps thundered into the village, down the steep hill from Cubert, through the gates and on up to the camp. Linda and I would rush out of the café, to the corner and wave and shout and we'd be thrilled when they tooted their horns and the soldiers all waved back, from the open backs of the lorries.

The extra trade they brought to the shops and Pub pleased everyone.

Off duty, the soldiers walked down from the camp usually still in their uniforms, although that did cause a fracas with the local lads a few times in the Treguth Pub if I remember rightly. Or they'd sit at the tables on the terrace outside the Café and Linda and I would play innocently amongst them. Great fun.

Linda went to Cubert school like me and we became inseparable.

We dressed similar and liked doing the same things. When we weren't at school, we could always find plenty to do. We'd walk up and help the farmer bring in the cows from his top field down to the farmyard for milking. He'd herd them down the main road using a big stick and he'd push his body against them to keep them in check, but they knew where they were headed and were pretty much well behaved.

I wasn't frightened by them until one trod on my foot in the cobbled farmyard as they were all milling around waiting to be taken into the milking shed.

No lasting damage, but it wasn't half sore. As a result, when the farmer offered one of us a lift onto the back of a cow to ride it down to the farmyard one time, I quickly said no, but have a go Linda, was eager to get a leg up from the farmer. There was nothing to hang on to, so she was bounced around as it waddled down the road.

We'd watch the farmer's wife hand churn the butter in the dairy or sometimes we'd drink milk straight from the cow when it was offered. Which to be honest wasn't very pleasant as it was always warm, but we didn't like to refuse for fear of upsetting him. But I loved collecting eggs from the field, where the hens roamed freely. We'd rummage around in the hedgerow up and down the field and squeal with delight when we found one and put it in our basket, even if it did have a feather or a bit of poo stuck to it. Some days there was loads, others not so many.

We'd go blackberry picking in late summer, picking the abundance of lush dark berries growing wild along the roadside. Careful not to prick our fingers on the thorns. Our little fingers would be black by the end, stained by the juice, if we squeezed too hard when prizing them off the bush. Mum would make my favourite, apple and blackberry pie with thick custard or Cornish cream which would melt over the top of the warm pie. Sometimes, Dad would take us mussel picking, prizing them off the rocks, for Mum to scrub and cook. But we were only allowed to do that when there was an 'R' in the month, he said.

Linda's Dad did all the cooking in their Café, wearing a navy blue and white striped apron tied around his ample waist. Sometimes if we were lucky, he'd give us the crispy bits from the bottom of the huge chip-pan that he couldn't sell to the customers and we'd smother them with tomato sauce and loads of salt, for our lunch. Frances, my sister worked there sometimes, waitressing, for extra pocket money.

Linda and I did nearly everything together, except one day, when she was playing in the sand dunes on her own, she was 'flashed' by a man in a Mac. Our parents were mortified and wouldn't let us out on our own for a while after that. I was so annoyed I'd missed it but didn't understand what 'being flashed' meant, just assumed for a long while after, that anybody who wore a Mac, was a 'flasher'.

Stepping out of our front gates at White Sails, across the dirt road and the small piece of wasteland used as a makeshift car park and we were on the vast sweep of sand dunes.

They were mountainous, totally obscuring any view of the beach and sea beyond.

Linda and I would spend hours exploring them, climbing up to the top, which was so hard as they were impossibly steep. With sand so silky soft that our feet just sunk into nothingness as we desperately tried to get a hold of the beach grasses as they swayed in the breeze, but usually ended up getting nowhere fast. When eventually we reached the top and got our breath back there was nothing better than rolling down the side of the dune, over and over, sand getting everywhere, eyes tight shut, so we didn't get any grit in them.

It was the best game ever. Then we'd do it all over again, slowly turning golden brown in the glorious sunshine. The beach, which was never overcrowded and the sea were just an extension of our home. If we weren't playing in the dunes, we'd have a picnic on the beach with family or visitors, paddle in the slow running freshwater stream, leading down to the sea, buckets ready to catch little fishes or crabs from the crystal-clear water.

Knitted swimsuits for Linda and I were the norm, which drooped southwards every time we got them wet. I never saw my Mum in a swimsuit. Although she had a lovely shapely figure, she didn't like showing too much, but still loved getting brown as she sat in the garden or on the beach.

She'd pull her full cotton skirt up just above her knees, showing her shapely calves and ankles and her strapless bandeau top guaranteed lovely, tanned shoulders. Her mid brown hair going a little lighter with the sun especially at the front where she'd use peroxide to give herself a blond streak every summer.

As kids we were constantly told how dangerous the sea could be especially if the tide was on the turn, so I was never allowed in on my own. Even when you were just paddling, you could sometimes feel the dangerous pull of the outgoing tide on your legs and knew not to go swimming, for fear of being swept out to sea.

When it was safe, Dad would usually come in with me and I'd laugh at him when he stripped off his top, as his face, neck and arms would be lovely and brown but you could clearly see where his vest had been, when he'd been working outside in the sun, as the rest of him would be pure white.

I loved catching a wave on my short plywood surfboard with its curved front. I'd walk out into the sea jumping up every time a wave came crashing towards me, until it reached about waist high, then I'd turn ready for the next big wave. Then lay my top half on the board and then as soon as the crest of the wave caught me, I'd lift my legs up and lay flat as the foaming white surf propelled me on the board towards the beach. If it was windy, the roar of the relentless huge waves would be deafening. I never did learn to swim as the sea was rarely calm enough.

The treacherous undercurrent caused several people to drown on Holywell beach, one summer alone. That's what prompted my Dad and the other villagers to seek finance from the local council to set up a Surf lifesaving club in the Bay and there was huge excitement when the small surf hut was built. Australian lifeguards appointed to patrol the increasingly popular beach.

Everyone wanted to sign up as volunteer life savers and we all had a go at practising the kiss of life on the life-size blow up doll, which at the time was bigger than me, causing much hilarity. My dear brother Cliff was so proud when he got his red and yellow life saver's swimwear, together with hat tied under the chin, typical Aussie style.

Often when someone tragically drowned, sadly the body wouldn't turn up for ages, if at all. But one day, I was exploring with my siblings, with Cliff rushing ahead as usual, into the cave by the Monkey rock. It was dark and damp.

Frances and I were concentrating hard trying not to slip on the slimy smelly bottle green seaweed which covered the rocks.

'Stop,' Cliff suddenly shouted, *'Don't come in, run and fetch Dad.'*

Luckily Mum and Dad were sitting in the dunes with our picnic lunch at the time, so we didn't have far to run. I found out later that there was a body caught up amongst the rocks. I wanted to stay and see what it was all about, but Mum bustled Frances and me home before we saw anything nasty.

Still a child, I was oblivious to the hard work that was involved in the tourist industry or understand the financial implications of not having a good season. I just knew that every summer, I'd be turfed out of my bedroom. During the winter, we'd have our pick of bedrooms from any one of the flats, but usually Frances and I shared the bedroom of the flat at the top of the stairs.

So, the large kitchen to the side of the property became our home for the Summer months, where we'd all eat, sleep and wash. Dad had built a toilet under the stairs. We washed in the sink each morning where Mum had washed the dishes the night before.

Frances and I had bunk beds in the corner surrounded by a curtain Mum had made, to shield us from the light as we were always the first to go to bed. Mum, Dad and Cliff had put-u-ups, that were taken down each morning and we ate in the same room.

We'd have a bath in one of the flats each Saturday in-between one lot of holidaymakers leaving and the next lot arriving. Everyone involved in the holiday trade was the same. Some people lived in garages, lofts, basements, caravans, just so that every possible nook and cranny could be used for paying guests. That became the norm for our family and then when the summer was over, you'd all spread out again and get your own bedroom back.

Mum and Dad had so many friends and relatives left behind in London and sorely missed, that there was an open invitation for them to come and stay, as long as they let us know, it was one family at a time and with the understanding they would have to rough it with the rest of us.

There was a room in front of the kitchen that Dad used for different things, mainly as storage and a workshop, his tools and spare furniture. When our non-paying visitors descended, this area was somehow miraculously turned into a dormitory with Mum arranging curtains or screens around beds to offer some privacy.

To be honest, everyone just mucked in together and it was great fun. We would never really know where we would end up sleeping, from one Summer to the next, depending how Dad had re-arranged the accommodation.

Alf and Kath Cull from Walthamstow were frequent visitors. Uncle Alf as I called him was Dad's cousin, but they were close, like brothers. Dad had a passion for fishing off the rocks of an evening, particularly for Mackerel. Mum and I would walk down at dusk with a hot flask of tea or soup and a sandwich and leave him to it. When he caught a few, we'd have them for our tea next day.

I'm not sure if it was the Mackerel or not, but something really upset Uncle Alf's tummy this one time when we were all sleeping in the same room. His to-ing and fro-ing to the toilet all night kept us all awake as did the associated pungent smells. But that was just part and parcel of our summer.

When the collecting tins came around for the RNLI, I would be dispatched around the village to knock on every door and collect as many coins as possible.

'Do I have to,' I'd whine, feeling anxious.

Mum and Dad seemed to put me into situations in a bid to cure me of my shyness, but it never worked very well. Having to knock on stranger's doors was traumatic, especially if the owner's reputation preceded them, such as the 'Colonel'. He lived at the top of the village just behind our house and I was terrified of him without ever having met the man. It was just hearing everyone talking about his grumpiness that scared me, so I don't think I ever did make it down his path.

One house I loved to visit though was that of Miss Missing. She lived in a bungalow, opposite the corner café, reached by a steep set of steps. Her exuberant black and white collie would run to greet me, backside and tail frantically wagging, trying to lick my face as I giggled, stroking her shiny coat.

We'd not had a dog before, so when Miss Missing's dog had pups, we took one and called her Mandy. It was a cross between a collie and a sausage dog. Not quite sure how that happened, but Mandy was a little yapper and because she was low on the ground, she'd nip at the back of your ankle, especially if she didn't like you.

If Linda was busy and I was a bit bored, I'd often jump in the car with Dad, while he was getting messages.

The Post Office in Cubert was a favourite. Just inside the door to the left was a display of leather purses. While Dad was busy at the counter, I'd look up and down the rows. Luxuriously soft and supple, I'd hold them in my hands, picking out a favourite, breathing in that distinctive earthy smell of new leather. I never did get around to owning one of those, but my love of all things leather, I believe stemmed from there.

Dad would call into the butchers and then we'd stop off for a tray of eggs from the house on the corner, on the way back home, which I'd have to perch on my lap, to make sure they didn't tip up and break.

Linda Gray and I were like twins, growing our hair at the same time, she had plaits, I had a ponytail, wearing similar dresses, losing teeth at the same time. We even did the three-legged race together on sports day, which was held in a field up Cubert where the sun-scorched grass had been cut short, leaving scratchy stubble behind. But that didn't stop us enjoying the egg and spoon and sack races on a lovely Summer's day.

But all that abruptly ended. The Gray family split up and Linda and her Mum went to live in Cubert for a while, I think with the Bennett family, if I remember rightly, so I mainly only saw her at school.

Ted and his daughter-in-law Bet continued to run the café and Mum and Dad stayed friends with them more so than with Kit, Linda's Mum.

It was a difficult time with split loyalties, but it resulted in my close friendship with Linda gradually petering out.

I'd suddenly lost my best friend.

Our Holy Well

When a little older, I'd be allowed to walk home the one and a half miles from Cubert school down the hill to Holywell, on my own. There were no pavements, just an overgrown footpath that wound its way along the roadside, my bare legs getting tickled by the long grass. Or stung by nettles which would then send me frantically searching for a dock leaf to rub away the stings.

Past Hartley's farm, which for years, I thought was the place that made Hartley's jam. Past Treguth Inn, where Seth, the one-armed man would be using a scythe to cut the grass verge.

Not sure if it were him, or the scary looking curved blade of the scythe that terrified me, but I would cross over the road to avoid walking past him. Most Sunday lunchtimes, I'd wait outside Treguth for my Dad, while he had had a couple of beers before our lunch. I'd be placated with a glass of lemonade and would be thrilled if I found more than one little blue bag of salt in my packet of Smiths crisps.

I'd nose in through the door trying to see the ties hanging from the beams that Dad had told me about and the cap badges of all the serving battalions that had been at Penhale Army camp, which had been accumulated by Lilian Dunkley, the landlady and her daughter Paddy.

To the right and a bit away from our property, down at the base of the vast sand dunes, the sand was excavated and used for making breeze blocks. The lorries would trundle past our front gates and we'd watch as the diggers dug away at the seemingly endless supply, fill the lorries and then they would trundle back, going the other way, taking the sand to the cement works, down Camborne way, where they made the blocks. There was never a sense of urgency, it wasn't intrusive or noisy and the sand just seemed to replenish itself from the enormous supply at hand.

Just past this area was the path we took to the Holy Well, where we'd always take visiting relatives or holidaymakers for a leisurely walk. 'Our' Holy well was found between Holywell and Cubert.

An old stone-built structure with pitched

roof, hidden away in deep matted undergrowth along an overgrown path. Crystal clear water trickled from rocks into a stone basin which overflowed into a little stream.

I thought it a magical place. There is still much debate on whether 'our' Holy well is the one the Bay was named after or if it's the well that can be found in the cave on the beach at low tide. I like to think it's 'ours'.

Across the fields, past the well, you could get to Polly Joke beach, a small, secluded bay inaccessible by road, therefore lovely and quiet.

We had holidaymakers that returned to stay in the flats year after year and some became almost part of the family and we'd go to the beach and swim and hang out with them.

One such family were the Coombes who lived in Borehamwood, not far from the Elstree film studios. Dilys and Eric and their four children, Anton, Megan, David and Glynis. Mum and Dad got on with them well. They were their kind of people, easy going and from the same neck of the woods.

After a few holidays with us, they eventually moved down to Cornwall and lived at Trencreek, where we'd regularly visit them. Anton, who had Cystic fibrosis sadly died in 1962. Megan was the first to emigrate to Australia, followed by Glynis, Eric and Dilys themselves and then finally David. After my Dad died, Mum visited them in Australia a few times. I'd had no direct contact with the family until we re-acquainted via the Newquay nostalgia page on Facebook a couple of years ago when they fondly reminisced about their stays at White Sails.

On Mum's last visit in the early 1990's, she left them a rose bush and now every year when it blooms, they send me a photo of the 'Doris Rose'. Lovely people and made Mum so welcome when she visited them.

Dad was always looking to make improvements and decided to build an extension at the side of White Sails for two new flats. He and Cliff spent months excavating the deep bank to start building. Dad did most of the work with my brother helping and learning the trades when he wasn't working as chef at the Holywell Bay hotel for the owner Mrs Mitchell and her son Nicky. Cliff had given up on his draughtsman training in London soon after we'd moved down to Cornwall, deciding that wasn't the career he wanted.

The extension was built of breeze blocks. When the shell was built, Dad was working on the first-floor timbers one day and fell through the rafters onto a large pile of breeze blocks on the ground floor.

'Cliff, quick, get the car, Dad's had a fall,' Mum shouted.

Dad couldn't move for a while with the shock and sheer panic that he had done himself a lot of damage. Mum made him a strong sweet tea and then she and Cliff took him to Newquay hospital. He didn't have an ounce of fat on him, as lean as a toothpick, so badly bruised all his ribs, but luckily no broken bones. He was black and blue and in agony for weeks and had to take a rubber ring to bed, just to try and get some comfortable sleep.

The Gough family lived next door. Geoff, Esme, daughter Sherie, a bit younger than me and a couple of older brothers, Nigel and Wimpy who Cliff hung around with sometimes. They had a Dalmatian dog that had puppies which regularly escaped into our garden causing mayhem.

'They're out,' someone would shout, and it would be all hands to the pump as we raced around the garden, trying to roundup these mischievous small balls of spotty dogs. Like slippery eels, they'd slither through your fingers, just as you thought you'd gotten a hold. They'd run in and out of your legs, tripping you up and then come and lick your face as you were laid flat out breathless on the grass.

Dad got friendly with Jack Philips who was working at the butcher's shop in Crantock. He and his wife Connie had moved from Catford, in South East London and Jack and Dad got on like a house on fire. Although Dad was an East end Londoner, he wasn't particularly outgoing, but if he took to you, then you became a good friend.

I developed a terrific crush on their younger son Peter, who was older than me. When they lived in Cubert, I'd walk up there on a Sunday on the pretence of saying hello to his Mum and Dad and have a cup of tea, just so I could hang out with the family and the focus of my adoration.

I'd always loved dancing and a love of music followed. When I got a small transistor radio, I used to listen to Radio Luxembourg, usually under the sheets when I was supposed to be sleeping, because the best programmes were on so late. That is if I could get a reception. I remember Barry Alldis, the DJ saying,

'Radio Luxemburg, your station of the Stars on 208 metres medium wave,' but I'd be lucky to hear all of that at once as the reception was so bad. I'd have to constantly twist and turn the radio every which way to get anything at all, it kept fading in and out, it'd drive me mad and was a constant frustration.

There was an advert where the address was *'Department One, Keynsham, spelt K-E-Y-N-S-H-A-M, Bristol.'* That address has stuck with me because I heard it so many times.

After Dad had finished the two new flats, he bought a chalet for the back garden for us all to sleep in, which was a fraction better than the makeshift sleeping arrangements we'd had previously in the kitchen, but not half as much fun.

My parents never hit any of us that I can remember, because there was never any need, we just did what we were told, too scared of any alternative and Dad only blew his top on the rarest of occasions.

Mum was a good cook, we had lovely home-made meals. But one time, Dad had bought a piece of beef from the butcher in Cubert and not sure if it was Mum's cooking, or the beef itself, but it was as tough as old boot. Dad was so annoyed, after just one mouthful, he opened one of the three little wooden windows above the sink in the kitchen and lashed it out.

Walking everywhere became our way of life in Cornwall, it was so hilly in parts and the bus service infrequent and there were so many lovely places to explore. Another place we always took visiting relatives to, was the 'The Lost Church'. We'd set off from White

Sails, walking up to Penhale Army camp and then over the fields towards Perranporth.

We were never sure if we'd find the church as it was in a dip and not marked in any way, so just luck of the draw if we stumbled across it.

The remains of this 6th century St. Piran's Oratory are believed to be one of the oldest places of Christian worship in Britain.

To protect the delicate remains from the constant bombardment from wind and sand, they were enclosed in a large concrete structure in 1910 and that was really all that we could see, but it was fascinating to envisage what was inside. The concrete structure was removed in 1980 and the site covered in sand to protect it further. It has been covered and uncovered various times since, to protect it and further restoration work is ongoing.

I'd never much liked Bonfire night. In Wembley I'd reluctantly be persuaded to go outside and hold a sparkler, whilst Dad set up the fireworks. But as soon as everything started whizzing and fizzing and soaring into the sky, I'd run inside to Mum, quite content to see everything through the window.

Therefore, I wasn't over keen when we were invited to the fireworks display one bonfire night at a farm in Cubert. All the locals were there. It was a cold crisp night, clear sky, twinkling stars and everyone was milling around before the fireworks started, chatting and drinking and I was in and out of the farmhouse, enjoying a piping hot baked potato to keep me warm, forgetting temporarily about what was to come. Eventually everyone mustered in the farmyard in front of the cowsheds, empty of cows thankfully and Mum and I stood well away, towards the back of the yard.

She wasn't that keen either. The fireworks were all laid out very neatly next to each other on the far wall in front of an open barn, at the opposite end to the cowsheds. We all stood in various degrees of anticipation. The younger ones thrilled as their sparklers lit up the dark yard before the main event started. Eventually someone lit the first firework and waited for the 'oohs' and 'aahs' from the crowd.

But something went horribly wrong. The anticipated 'oohs' and 'aahs' turned into screams, shouts and shrieks of panic.

Instead of the firework going skywards, it went sideways, reaching out to hug the firework next to it, which then did the same to its neighbour, like dominoes, because all the fireworks had been neatly placed beside each other on the wall. The whole lot went up and all hell broke loose.

Fireworks were jumping every which way except up towards the sky, where they were supposed to go. There were Catherine wheels spinning horizontally, out of control into the crowd, rockets made a beeline for the cowsheds and the barn was filled with spaceships, spinning around and around with nowhere to go. Everyone scattered, trying to avoid the mayhem.

Mum and I being the closest to the cowsheds dived in there for shelter oblivious to the fact that it hadn't been cleaned out and was still full of cow muck. Well we'd run right into it before realising and suddenly stopped. Mum was in further than me where the manure was deepest and promptly ran back out screeching. Much more concerned with the smelly mess now attached to her legs, than she was with the dangerous, out of control fireworks.

Emerging from the shed minus one shoe, she was not about to go back in to retrieve it.

Luckily and I don't know how, no-one was injured that night and the talking point thereafter was not just about the disaster of the fireworks, but the hilarious recounting of Mum's lost shoe. She never did get it back, but I don't think she would ever have worn those shoes if she had. They would have gone straight in the bin!

Dad would drive into Newquay and collect holidaymakers that were due to stay with us from the railway station if they didn't have a car. One time, he hadn't secured their cases well enough on the roof rack and as he was driving back, one of the cases fell off and the lady's unmentionables were spread all over the road, outside Cubert Post Office. Just as well it was the start of their holidays and they were in a good mood and able to laugh it off.

He had a Lea Francis estate car by this time. Quite unique with its wooden frame and anytime we'd pass another on the road, Dad and the other driver would always wave, flash their lights, or toot their horn as there were so few of them about. He would always pick up hitchhikers, if we had the room as they were a very common sight, normally with huge backpacks. One time he picked up what he soon realised was a tramp and the car stank to high heaven for days afterwards. He was a bit choosy who he picked up after that.

The dunes protected our house from the full-on elements of the sea, but you could still hear the roar of the waves, the squawk of gulls overhead and taste the saltiness in the air. I spent lazy days roaming around the dunes opposite our house or picking buttercups, holding the flower under my chin, to see if it glowed yellow, proving I loved butter.

Cliff went all goggle eyed and star struck when three models, including David McCallum's then wife Jill Ireland, came to do a bikini modelling shoot on the sand dunes opposite our house. Cliff was smitten. Didn't leave our garden all day.

I raced across the dunes when Radio Caroline visited the bay and I heard them on the radio, urging people to come out and wave. Side-stepping all the deep and dangerous rabbit burrows, I reached the cliff edge just as the boat disappeared around the headland towards Newquay. But I still waved frantically.

I'd wait for Frances and Cliff by the surf lifesaving hut, for them to finish working at the Holywell Bay hotel.

'Hi, Ho, Hi, Ho, it's off to the beach we go,' would ring out as they and their mates would appear through the middle of the sand dunes, singing loudly.

It's so easy to spot pictures or photos of the Holywell beach because of the unmistakeable sight of the huge twin Gull rocks that sit out to sea.

They can't be seen from the village, it's only when you take the path down by the stream that hugs the cliffs and round the bend of the sand dunes that they suddenly come into view.

Made so famous by the recent Poldark series, much of which was filmed on this beach.

Living in the peace, safety, stillness and tranquillity of Holywell Bay was the most magical of childhoods. One I so very much enjoyed but didn't fully appreciate at the time but cherish the memories of now.

Being constantly outdoors, became our way of life. We were never short of something to do. With no passing traffic, no crowds, and with the beach, sea, and sand dunes at our fingertips to explore and enjoy.

But my life changed again when I was eleven. Mum decided my shyness needed to be even further challenged, so she sent me to even more dance classes. Then I did the unthinkable as far as she was concerned.

I passed my eleven plus!

Blue Lagoon...Take One

'One, two, three, one, two, three, one, two, three,' Norman repeated, as we all lined up in a row behind him as he showed us for the first time the basic box steps for the waltz.

Mum had despatched me yet again to dance classes. This time to Ballroom and Latin American with Norman and Maizie Tyler at the Blue Lagoon in Newquay, on a Saturday morning. I still loved to dance at every opportunity at home, but she must have gotten fed up with seeing the same routine Linda and I performed for her. I'd make Mum sit on a chair outside White Sails in the sunshine, while we pranced around to Cliff Richard's 'Living Doll' or Pat Boone's Speedy Gonzales or whatever was on the radio.

I like to think it was because she thought I had a talent for dance, but it could have been just to get me out of her and Dad's hair for a few hours on what was the busiest day of their week and all that the frenzy of a 'Summer season Saturday' entailed. Holidays were seven, or fourteen-day affairs, none of this weekend break or three-or four-day malarkey.

Hence, everything happened on the one day. A day of gushing goodbyes, hoping the departing holidaymakers would book again for the following year. Then a turmoil of washing sheets, changing towels, sweeping floors, scrubbing sinks, within a few snatched hours, making ready to warmly welcome the next onslaught of guests with sometimes only minutes to spare. Dad would drop me off at the Blue Lagoon, then come back a few hours later to pick me up. Often crammed in the car with guests he'd picked up at Newquay station, if they hadn't come far or got an early train.

Buses back to Holywell were few and far between and they thought I was too young to find my own way home anyway.

The 'Blue' as I came to know it later, was on Cliff Road in Newquay, opposite the Sussex grill which had the most mouth-watering spit-roasted chickens in the window, from which the heavenly smell would waft out the open door. The Great Western Hotel was next door to the 'Blue', with a road in-between leading to the steep hill down to the Great Western Beach that a few years later would become my second home.

Maizie and Norman were professional dancers and looked the part. Maizie with her coiffured blond hair piled high and Norman looking dapper in his suit. At first, I just didn't want to be there. The thought that I'd have to get into an up close and personal hold with someone in the ballroom dances filled me with dread. I was pleased there weren't many boys in the class. Often, it would be with another girl, which was less daunting.

However, occasionally, it would be with Norman himself, sending me into that familiar panic of sweaty awkwardness and nerves.

'Stop looking at the floor Denise,' Maizie would tell me, as I struggled constantly to make eye contact with my partner, whoever it was.

The whole experience of those first classes was excruciating to be honest, but after a while, I really got into the dancing and loved it.

As you walked into the Blue Lagoon, the stage was in front of you and there were columns decorated like Palm trees, at regular intervals across the dance floor appearing to hold up the ceiling. It was always a bit dim, with little or no lighting except from the row of windows high up on the sea facing side of the building to the right. But with the amount of times I must have gone red with embarrassment, the low lighting suited me fine.

I liked the ballroom dances, the waltz and the foxtrot but preferred the Latin American salsa and cha, cha, cha, where it was less in hold which was considerably better. Much more freedom.

After a couple of months into the class when most of us had grasped the basics and at the height of the Summer season, Maizie asked if we'd all like to attend the regular Saturday night dance for a demonstration. Well, the thought of having to dance in front of strangers with everybody looking on, terrified the life out of me, so I didn't mention it at home. But the following week Maizie mentioned it to Dad when he came to pick me up.

He thought it a great idea, so dressed in the pink dress with a white raised embossed pattern on it and white bow at the neck, that Mum had made me for the class, off I went, when the night arrived. Completely traumatised that we'd have to give a demonstration. I didn't have a clue what that meant.

As well as us learners, there were locals and holidaymakers and after there had been a few slow ballroom dances and then a jive and cha, cha, cha, which left everyone a bit breathless and needing a rest, we all returned to our seats positioned around the outside of the dance floor. It was a full house.

After a few minutes lull, the band struck up again and the Band leader announced...

'Now, what you've all been waiting for, it's demonstration time....'

I didn't hear any more, but slowly and reluctantly stood up out of my seat.

'What are you doing?' the girl sitting next to me said, as she yanked me back down again.

Bewildered, I looked around to see other bemused faces looking at me, at which point Maizie and Norman flounced onto the floor in all their finery. She was in a beautiful pale blue frock with bejewelled bodice and huge skirt made up of petticoat, upon petticoat of Tulle, which I'd seen Mum use lots of times when she made costumes for customers in London.

The huge, layered skirt bounced around as she walked and with Norman in his Tails, they looked just like the dancers I loved to watch on Come Dancing commentated by Peter West. As they glided around the floor to their first dance, a Waltz, I was thankful it wasn't me everyone was looking at yet ashamed for thinking that when they had mentioned a 'demonstration', it would be us learners giving it.

How stupid was I. I must have been quite good though in the end, because I passed several dance exams in both Ballroom and Latin. It was our participation in the regular Flora dances that took place through Newquay town centre, during the Summer months, that I really enjoyed though.

They'd taught us a routine to the Flora dance music. There were loads of floats and bands and dancers and people dressed up and it was such a fun time. Especially as by that time my confidence in my dancing in front of strangers had grown a little and I enjoyed taking part. We'd muster up on Narrowcliff and the long procession would start. There was an order to it and our place would be to follow one of the bands, so we could keep in time with the music.

All the girls were dressed in a pink frock and the boys in short trousers and shirts. We'd hop and skip and twirl and move forward down the street, sometimes having to mark time, because there was a blockage up front somewhere. With people packed both sides of the streets, waving and clapping as we passed, it was a great feeling, knowing that they liked what you were doing. I was fiercely proud of living in such a beautiful place, knowing that they, as holidaymakers would soon have to go home.

We'd pass the big impressive old hotels on the left of Narrowcliff, with their magnificent views out to the Atlantic. The Bristol, Bella Vista, Cliffdene, Marina, Tolcarne, St. Brannocks, Penolver, Beresford and the Crigga Bay. Past the 'Blue' onwards towards the Victoria Hotel and down into the town towards the Killacourt, the lush green space in the centre of town.

We would do it whatever the weather so sometimes we'd be soaking wet by the end. The most memorable occasion though was when we were on a float and able to dress up. I was going to be an Indian Squaw, so Mum made me this tan coloured dress with fringing around the bottom. I had a wig on with plaits, that I haven't a clue where that came from and my sister made me up to look tanned like a red Indian. I loved it. I was in my element.

I was so full of confidence that night because it wasn't me on show. I was playing a role, being someone else. I waved to the crowds, sung along to the music, smiling and laughing. It was a brilliant night.

I was with Maizie and Norman a few years, but as I became a teenager, I had other interests, of which, gazing at the surfers on Great Western beach, became the main one.

As the 1960s wore on, ballroom dances lost their appeal, so the 'Blue' transformed itself into Newquay's hot nightspot. Where a much younger generation would gyrate to the sound of Motown bands, big name singers as well as local groups and disco music. The whole place was spruced up with a bar built up top overlooking the sea.

So, my next encounter with this popular dance venue, when a teenager, soon became a far cry from my first 'Blue' experience.

It was where I was to get myself into all sorts or trouble!

Mind your Grammar

'*Nothing wrong with the secondary modern,*' Mum argued. '*It's been good enough for Cliff and Frances,*' she added, as I tried to argue back.

There were various times in my life when I know I was a huge disappointment to my Mum and the first memorable occasion came, when I passed that eleven plus to go to Newquay Grammar school. Any other mother would have been proud and delighted, but not mine. Her philosophy was that hard work got you everything in life and she viewed higher education, as a complete waste of time.

I believe that this was the one and only time that my Dad was able to put his foot down in my favour. When the long list of required uniform and equipment arrived, off we reluctantly went to Foster Trinimans, on East street, the only specialist shop in Newquay. Up to this point she'd made all my clothes and knitted all my sweaters, so having to buy a completely new school uniform from an expensive shop, mortified her and the whole experience was excruciating, for me, her, as well as for the poor salesman.

The uniform was a grey pleated skirt, grey blazer with maroon piping and a grey hat with maroon ribbon trim, which I had a terrible job keeping in place with my mop of thick frizzy hair. I had a maroon striped tie for Treffry, the 'house' I was to go into. The other school 'houses' were yellow for Restormal, green for Edgcumbe and blue for Caerhays.

Having to buy the hockey stick was the last straw though and she positively refused when it came to the discretionary lacrosse stick, which was just as well as I never did get the hang of that game.

Mind you she got her own back. I was nervous enough about my first day at Newquay Grammar, but she had insisted on giving me the most viciously tight perm I had ever had. Although I had naturally thick wavy hair, it had a mind of its own, so perming was her way of controlling it. Nobody at school spoke to me for two weeks until the unmistakeable and overpowering fumes from the Twink perm lotion had dispelled.

Despite that embarrassing start, I made some good friends and by this time, the early sixties, Mum and Dad had bought a brand new bungalow in Middleton Crescent, Newquay so that we three children could be near school, work and friends and I think to stop Dad having to ferry us into the town all the time.

They were still running White Sails as a business so would go back and forth every day. As well as the flats, Mum had opened a little tea shop in a hut Dad had built her in the garden at Holywell and she sold ice creams, trays of tea and her home-made doughnuts.

She'd make the dough each evening and leave it to prove overnight and then fry them off in the morning, douse them in sugar and inject strawberry jam into the middle with a syringe.

They were so popular, that she could never make enough. Customers would enjoy them sitting around the tables with umbrellas Dad had erected on the lawn.

So, once again we were living between two houses and although most of our time was spent in

Newquay, at weekends we'd all go down to White Sails and enjoy the beach and surfing in the sea at Holywell.

Middleton Crescent was a small quiet cul-de-sac in Trenninick, a mile or so out of the centre of town, with uninterrupted views overlooking green fields and the Gannel beyond. I don't think Mum and Dad ever had much intention of staying there because, unusually for them, they didn't do much with the garden, except for a few strawberry plants down the bottom. It was all lawn apart from that, no vegetable patch, no flower beds or rockery or landscaping, so perhaps they only ever intended to make it a brief stopover.

However, Mum still insisted on having an Aga in the small kitchen. The lounge was L shaped with picture windows looking out onto the garden. My sister and I shared a room, with Mum and Dad next door and Cliff in a small room of his own up the four stairs opposite the bathroom.

We settled there for a few years, I'd sometimes walk home from Grammar school with Pat Roberts who lived just around the corner on Mellanvrane Lane, next to Mr Gerber's house, our Headmaster. I'd be mortified if I'd see him of a weekend as I passed by his garage, muttering *'Hello Sir,'* as I hurried past.

Jenny Critchley was my first good friend at Grammar school. She was petite, tiny in fact, with fine fair hair and she and her twin brother Rafe were in my class. Her parents owned the Corisande Manor Hotel up Pentire, which was an unusual but imposing building like a Gothic castle, with ornate balconies and having glorious views overlooking the river Gannel.

I visited a few times, to play, and found it a little bit creepy with a warren of rooms. With its dark wood original features, endless nooks and crannies and creaky floorboards. Her Dad, Major Critchley scared me a little, so one time we hid from him in a huge wooden chest in one of the rooms, which he wasn't too pleased about when he eventually found us.

Elizabeth Littlejohn was another good pal. She was tall, slim, pretty, and popular. Her Dad was in the Royal Air Force, stationed at St. Mawgan Air base. For her 12th birthday in 1963 Liz invited a few of us to her house for a sleepover. They had a large house in the picturesque village of St. Mawgan, so we were all in the same room, chatting half the night away. On the Saturday after our tea her Mum had made us Baked Alaska. I'd never tasted anything like it, with hot golden meringue encasing smooth cool ice-cream. I thought it was marvellous as we watched the Rolling Stones on the TV.

At that time, I'd get confused between the Beatles and the Stones, but that didn't last long, and the Beatles became the centre of my world.

'What a racket,' Dad used to say. *'They'll never last,'* as I wrote to their fan club asking them how to make a chip butty. We were Southerners, you see!

Liz's Dad was posted to Aden for two years soon afterwards, so the whole family went with him. Liz and I wrote regularly on those unmistakable pale blue air mail letters, where I had to write in miniature to cram everything in and then fold up carefully, licking the sides to seal.

That first Christmas in Middleton Crescent was one I always remember. I'm not saying that Mum hadn't tried, prior to that one, but this one sticks in my memory, for all the right reasons. There was a huge tree in the corner, by the picture window with coloured tinsel and glass baubles hanging from every branch. I had loads of presents on Christmas morning to unwrap. They were all small things, like pencil cases and socks and colouring books and crayons, but I was overwhelmed by the sheer volume of little parcels there were with my name on. I was thrilled.

Mum was easy to buy for at Christmas and birthdays, as her love of the real Turkish delight was endless. It came in a wooden drum, containing squares of a mixture of rose and lemon flavour, dusted in icing sugar. Then there was her mantra of moisturise,

moisturise, moisturise, for which she relied on using Oil of Ulay, which came in that distinct pink bottle, always present on her dressing table.

Dad was a bit more difficult, but his passion for Golden Virginia tobacco which came in green and gold 2 oz tins and red Rizla cigarette papers, could always be relied on, to bring a smile from him. His other passion was a blond singer of the time called Kathy Kirby, who seemed to mesmerise him every time she came on the tele. Couldn't quite get her for him under the Christmas tree. Then again, Mum would have been a might upset if I had! Mum couldn't moan though as she'd be equally glued to the tele every time Liberace appeared, mesmerised by his over the top flamboyancy and outrageous costumes.

By the time I'd reached my teens in 1964, my sister Frances, six years older and my brother Cliff, eight years older were well into their working lives and I was far too young to hang around with them. I wasn't yet allowed out much on my own and if I did go visiting, to friend's houses, I'd get ferried there and back. Ironic, when I'd been allowed to go to the shops in Wembley and explore in Holywell, on my own, from an early age. So not sure if, as I got older and was taking an interest in boys, it was me they didn't trust, or everyone else.

But occasionally in Summer, I'd be allowed to go into Newquay with friends on my own during the day and if I wasn't feeling up to climbing Trenance Hill, I'd walk the long way around, under the viaduct, up the path to Quarry Park road, past the Christadelphian Hall, behind my school and then cut up towards the station, passing the Gay Cavalier pub.

Before the obsession with surfers had kicked in, me and my friends would go down the harbour and watch local lads jump off the harbour wall, at high tide.

We got used to the strong fishy smell that was always evident from the busy working harbour. We'd walk through the town stopping to look at the tortoises in the garden of the cottage, along from Gill's fish and chip shop.

Or get frustrated by the slow dawdling holidaymakers as they leisurely strolled down the main streets, blocking our path. No urgency to get anywhere. We'd stride past them, deliberately looking in their direction, saying loudly...

'Wish these flipping emmets would all go home.' Knowing full well, they wouldn't know what we were talking about and that emmets was a term us locals called holidaymakers.

Or we'd giggle if someone got divebombed by a seagull, ending up with that horrible white smelly poo in their hair.

When Mum wanted us out of *her* hair while she cleaned up, I'd be dispatched into town with Dad, which to be honest I didn't mind as I hated her hoovering, lifting of chairs, being moved around or having to lift my feet every five minutes. Being out with Dad was much better although it did get a bit boring, even with him sometimes.

He'd be in his element visiting all his local haunts for his DIY, building material and gardening needs. On a good day we'd only visit a few but on a bad day, we'd do the full set. Huxtables and Electrical Services on East Street first, Westlakes on Bank street with its eclectic selection of horse brasses, camping gear and surfboards amongst a mass of other stuff and the unmistakable smell of Paraffin. Then Bickers on the Whim for wood. F.C. West on Tower road, then the Paint spot in Wesley yard, finishing at Bulmores at the bottom of St. Georges road, which had its own distinct aroma and where he'd buy distemper, his go to paint for a variety of uses.

Might not have always been in that order depending how the mood took him. Can't recall there being a one-way system then, as we were able to drive down Bank street as well as park right outside the places he needed to visit.

If Mum and Dad did ever want to buy new furniture, which was quite a rarity, the go-to place was John Nance who had several showrooms around town.

Perhaps I'd hung around with Dad for too long when he was sawing wood at home in his shed and the smell and dust would linger in the air or the curled-up shavings would carpet the shed floor, but I found all the different smells of those shops familiar and somehow comforting. Then we'd head home, usually with a carload of stuff.

Dad was forever building, mending, or fixing so had to keep his supply constantly topped up, whether it be wood, paint, nails and even the odd tin of live maggots for his fishing trips. Not sure where he bought those from. He'd keep them in his shed in an old Golden Virginia tin, with holes punched in the top until he was ready to go fishing with Cliff. Regular haunts were up the reservoir or off the rocks or the beach.

He worked for Fred Bickers on and off over the years as a joiner, during the Winter or when money was a bit tight, but he liked being his own boss too much to make it permanent.

I would watch Dad do jobs around the house, not realising how useful the many tips would be that I was picking up. Like how to paste, hang and match wallpaper, how to paint and clean paint brushes or how to wire an electric plug and change a fuse. 4 by 4 meant something completely different to me back then, nothing to do with cars. Because 4 by 4 or 4 be 4 as it would sound when Dad said it, plus 4 be 2 and 2 be 2 were all sizes of lengths of wood. These would regularly be sticking out of the car window because they were too long to fit inside the car.

I had to be a contortionist sometimes as the planks rested on the back seat and stuck out the front passenger window, giving me little room to sit anywhere.

On Saturday afternoons in the Winter, I'd read my magazine that I'd bought in Menzies on Bank street, while Dad was in Westlakes. Bunty or June, then Jackie when I got a bit older, progressing on to the New Musical Express when my attentions turned towards the Beatles as they exploded onto the music scene.

Mum and I would watch an old black and white film, hoping it would be a Fred Astaire musical and then the wrestling at four o clock. I loved watching Giant Haystacks, Jackie Pallo with his blond ponytail and Mick McManus throw each other across the ring and in all sorts of the most painful looking holds. Little did I know that most of it was put on for the cameras.

Then Dad would check his Vernons Pools coupon at 5 o clock, or the Treble Chance as it was known, marking it off, to see if he'd won us a fortune. I can still hear the slow deep, melodious voice of the announcer. Brighton and Hove Albion, two, then a slight pause before... Leicester city, one.

Mum would cook us Cod's roe for our tea that she'd bought in the fish shop down Beachfield Avenue, next to the church. She fried it both sides until it was golden and lovely and crisp. She'd sometimes buy a wing of Skate for herself, dunk it both sides in flour and then fry it. There was one large flat bone going right through the centre, so you scraped the lovely white fish off both sides.

But that was Mum's special treat as it was too expensive for us all to have and Dad was easy going, he didn't mind what he ate.

Having said that though he did have some favourites that he made for himself. A hot fruity curry, which I liked as well, but then there was the brawn, which none of us could stomach. I think it was more to do with how he made it. Without warning, a couple of hairy pig's trotters would suddenly appear in the fridge. Then came the lengthy process of him cooking them, stripping the meat, which he put in aspic jelly and left to set. Being from the East End of London, I think that brawn reminded him of the jellied eels he'd enjoyed in his youth.

Mum's weakness was for sliced banana and sugar sandwiches or a dish of strawberries in summer with caster sugar liberally sprinkled over the top, irrespective of whether they were naturally sweet or not.

Like Dad, she was always on the go, a real grafter like him, doing or mending or fixing or sewing. Buying anything new though, went totally against the grain and usually, I was her accomplice in her quest for make do and mend being the order of the day.

How I longed for something that wasn't pre-used, pre-worn or pre-loved.

How I longed for her to buy something *new*!

Growing up

'Lot number twelve, a box of ornaments and trinkets. Come on now who'll start the bidding?' said the auctioneer, looking around the room, trying to catch someone's eye.

I was praying Mum wouldn't put her hand up. Just this once. She couldn't resist a box that she deemed to be a potential treasure trove of goodies. She was nothing but optimistic.

If it was the school holidays and it was a Friday, then she'd drag me up to John Julian's sale rooms at the top of Crantock street. Driving around with Dad was a bit of a chore but going to the Auctions with Mum was excruciating. You could go and have a rummage through all the sale lots on offer that day and make a note of the lot numbers you wanted to bid on.

Then a bit later the auction would start. To be fair she was a dab hand at bidding, even if half the things she bought were rubbish. I was terrified of moving in case I inadvertently bid on something I shouldn't, just by raising my arm to brush the hair away from my face.

Sometimes though, the boxes would have a hidden gem inside, if not it would go back into the next auction. She'd buy old bits of furniture to strip down and re-varnish or re-cover and the fetching brass angel in flight she found in one of the boxes, one time, was one of the rare objects that Dad liked, so they kept that for future use.

The smell in the sale rooms was not one that I remember fondly. It was musty, dusty and you felt like you needed a good wash when you got home for fear that you'd caught something nasty.

What was nice about days with Mum though, was that we'd sometimes just have a mooch around the shops, calling in for a pasty, and the only place to go for those would be Mathews Café.

The unmistakeable aroma escaping from Mr Mathew's pasty shop would make you salivate before you ever reached the entrance to the little narrow café tucked away on a corner in Central Square. This was a gem that you didn't share with holidaymakers as the locals wanted it all for themselves, but all too often there was a queue stretching out into the street. You'd be mortified if the rows of pasties in the hot cabinet disappeared before your very eyes.

However, when you did manage to get your hands on one of these little beauties, it was pure heaven. They were small but so tasty with the flakiest of pastry, packed with soft onion and potato, oozing with juicy meat, always piping hot, which, if you weren't careful, would burn your tongue in your eagerness to take that first delectable bite.

I can taste them now!

We'd walk up past the Sailors Arms and sit overlooking the bowling green on Fore street, keeping one eye on nearby squawking scavenging seagulls while we devoured our pasties.

Then we'd have a nose in the windows of Rumbles leather shop and Kay Whites on Fore street, on the way back, never going in as they were beyond our means, so Mum said. But we'd have a mooch around Cole and sons at the bottom of Crantock street, a double fronted shop that sold a mix of household and clothing items from carpets to hosiery.

I'd be transfixed by the pulley that transported the money around the shop and catapulted it up into presumably the office on the next floor. We'd get something for Dad's tea from Ayres the butchers, a big bag of pick and mix from Woolworths next door on Bank street, then call into Home and Colonial for cheese and a few bits.

Mum would have to drag me away from Lennards shoe shop, next to Cornish Silk, before we briefly browsed around Hawke and Thomas at the dress materials, just up the road on the corner of Beachfield Avenue, before heading home.

If Mum wasn't going to the Auction rooms, she'd drag me along to a jumble sale at St. Michael's church. As a staunch supporter of 'make do and mend', she'd buy things at the jumble, just to take the zip out to re-use or take the buttons off to add to her ever-expanding button box.

She'd be delighted if we found home-made sweaters for her to unpick, then wash the wool to knit up into something new. Mum wasn't called second-hand Rose for nothing.

Frances loved horse riding, going regularly to the stables behind Trenance boating lake. The woman who ran it lived at Treninnick farm, at the top of Mellanvrane Lane. Mum thought it a good idea if I went with her. I was frightened just going into the stable yard, the horses towering above me with legs nearly as tall as me. I was put on a small horse and Frances lent me her riding hat.

We set off down the Gannel in a line and within minutes, the hat, which was much too big, slipped over my eyes. I was terrified of letting go of the reins, to lift it back up, so rode on blind for a while before Frances noticed and came back to sort me out. Never again.

Lots of things happened in the three years we lived at the bungalow, for us siblings.

Frances my sister, started work for Jenkins on Fore street. It was a spooky building, particularly where she worked up in the eaves, so she didn't stay there long.

She moved to the knitting factory as a finisher, up the top of Crantock street, next to the John Julian's auction rooms. They provided garments for Madame Hawke opposite the station on Cliff road. After passing her shorthand and typing exam, she moved into the office there before finally moving onto Beresford motors on East street, doing invoicing before becoming the office secretary.

That was where she first noticed her husband to be, Alan Greenland. He worked for D.P.May and he'd deliver fruit and veg all over town, But when he delivered to Rawle's fish shop and the Penunda café just along from the Motors, he'd always take a bit of extra time to walk past several times trying to catch a glimpse of Frances, she found out later. But she didn't meet him properly until one night when she was out having a drink in the Treguth Inn in Holywell.

Alan was with his three great pals, George Hautot, Frank Dungey and Cyril Hubber. Alan was the smartest dresser out the four, so that's why she took a shine to him and probably the fact that he had a nippy red MG helped. George's yellow Cadillac with horns on the front fender must have been a bit showy for her, I think.

Alan would pick her up in Middleton Crescent and Mum wouldn't be at all amused because he'd park at the top of the road, not drive right to the door and she thought this most disrespectful. The reason though was because it was a new crescent, the road hadn't been made up and with his car being so low to the ground, he was worried it would get damaged by all the rubble.

When he came for tea or just dropped Frances off and popped his head in to say hello to us all and they'd be standing by the front door, kissing and cuddling saying goodnight, I'd purposely go to the loo or to the bedroom to stop their canoodling mid flow, just to annoy her.

It was where my brother Cliff loved and lost Ushi his German girlfriend whom he'd met whilst working as a chef. She was tall, with cropped short hair and always wore plain v neck sweaters, which made her look a bit masculine.

She was a no-nonsense type of a person, but nice none the less. Cliff visited her family back in Germany and all seemed to be going well, then she suddenly left and returned home for good.

Cliff was heartbroken. He'd be on the phone for hours trying to get through to her or her family but neither they nor she wanted to speak to him, and it was all my parents could do to stop him from going over there. Something serious must have happened, but I never did get to find out what.

It was where I really started to take an interest in boys and after going to a birthday party for Richard, the son of the local reporter, Mr Ravilious, I started getting phone calls from one of the boys that was there, much to the dismay of my parents.

The different groups of boys that started to impact my world at that time, were easily identifiable.

There were the local lads who you'd sat next to at school. Who'd tried to snog you on the back seat of the coach as you'd gone on that school trip for the roller skating down Redruth. Whose antics sometimes made them seem years younger than you, even though they were your peers. But with whom you felt comfortable and safe and could have a good laugh.

There were the local surfers, who you'd followed around from beach to beach, because you had a crush on most of them, with their tousled hair, athleticism, and bronzed bodies, who were so obsessed with their sport, they hardly gave you a second glance.

There were the hotel workers who had an unmistakable air of confidence and self-assuredness bordering on arrogance. Because they thought, being from the big cities and street wise they could buy and sell the Yocals. Who, for a night out, dressed immaculately, in their made to measure suits. They seemed older, different, more than a little scary, yet exciting at the same time.

Lastly came the holidaymakers. You could spot them a mile away, with their lily-white bodies, pristine stiff shorts with a crease down the front. T-shirt with the label hanging out the back and their Jesus sandals and socks if they hadn't had time to buy that first pair of flip-flops. But it was the way they carried a Malibu board, or tried to, that really gave them away.

They couldn't quite master the art of carrying the board under one arm, effortlessly like the professionals. They hugged it with both arms, one each side. Unnatural and ungainly. If they were on the beach, they'd give it up as a bad job and drop the rear end onto the sand and just drag the board into the water.

God forbid if they were anywhere near you in the town as they manhandled it down Bank street, not quite getting the balance right. It would swing every which way, knocking anyone down in close proximity, like skittles!

This deepening observation and interest in boys was the reason behind my weekly fights with my Mum, as I started to take more notice about my appearance. I was the last in my class to wear a bra and when she did eventually relent, ended up buying me an ill-fitting cotton monstrosity. Looking back, it must have been the protype for that extremely pointed outfit Madonna wore on her Blond ambition tour.

Middleton Crescent was also where I 'became a woman'. All Mum did, was give me a hug. She'd never given me 'the talk' on anything to do with sex education. I'd learnt more from girls at school who had already been through it, but I was still a bit scared when it happened to me. No wonder I was naïve!

It was where I used to wait on the doorstep, having arrived from school only to find that they weren't yet home from Holywell Bay. I'd wait for ages, hours sometimes and Mrs Loveridge from next door, who was a teacher at Tretheras school, would take me in for a cup of tea, feeling sorry for me, but still I wouldn't be allowed to have a key.

One such time I was in the back garden waiting for them, when a local Labrador wandered in and started to hump my leg. Didn't realise at the time what it was trying to do and struggled to prize it's legs apart, which were wrapped tightly around one of mine. It was scary.

I knuckled down at school, still walking home, but now, with a huge satchel of homework. I'd cut through Trenance caravan park sometimes. There was a makeshift path just after the viaduct going up into the park and I would wonder who lived in the permanent mobile homes with their immaculate flowering gardens. I thought it a lovely peaceful place to live.

Dad would sometimes pick me up in whatever car he was passionately restoring at the time. I was mortified if anyone saw me, when he had an old Daimler that resembled an ice cream van. The previous owner obviously having a sense of humour, had painted the top half bright yellow and the bottom half bright blue.

Mum would take me to the Astor cinema on Narrowcliff or the Pavilion cinema in the Crescent to see West Side Story, or the Sound of Music or Zulu, or whatever was the film of the moment. Then, if it was a special treat, we'd call into Macari's, down Gover Lane, an American style diner with its round stools at the counter. Where I'd demolish a scrumptious ice-cream sundae known as a knickerbocker glory, that was served in a tall glass with a long spoon, to scoop out every last mouthful.

As a family, we'd go for walks of a Sunday, out of season, when it was quiet, but still decent weather, through the town, on the beach, down to the Harbour or up to the Huer's hut.

The early sixties sort of came and went for me. I didn't appreciate the significance of the assassination of JFK, or the first manned space mission.

However, when the Beatles arrived on the scene, I was a teenager, beginning to blossom. Newquay was buzzing by this time and the once sleepy Cornish town was fast becoming a bustling cosmopolitan Mecca for young people from all over the country.

It was where I transitioned from child to teenager and my thoughts were muddled between wanting desperately to grow up, yet still being afraid there was something lurking in the wardrobe.

I'd close my eyes tight once I'd got into bed and pull the bedclothes right over my head and not dare to peep out. Middleton Crescent was my gateway to adolescence and a stepping-stone for my parents to take us on to the next stage of our adventures.

So it was, that by the mid-sixties, my parents got itchy feet again and the next chapter in our lives was going to be running a guest house.

They sold White Sails to Eve and Arthur Potter, who built another couple of flats on the left-hand side of the building. Mum and Dad and I visited them a few times after it was built and I believe they also bought the Corner café, not sure if that was from the Gray family or if they had moved on by then.

The bungalow in Middleton Crescent was sold to the Stanton family who also became firm friends. Both properties were sold so Mum and Dad could buy Treninnick House, which lay just opposite the entrance to the Crescent. It was a beautiful old Cornish farmhouse, part of which is mentioned in the Doomsday book. It lay in a dip, partially hidden by huge trees and had walls three feet thick.

The bungalow had obviously been a bit too normal for them, so the running of a guest house and taking in holidaymakers for Dinner, Bed and Breakfast was to be our next family adventure.

The fun and frolics that came with that though, is another story entirely!

Don't tell the Guests

The roast potato toppled off the serving dish and plopped onto the floor, as Dad, on a mission as usual had taken the corner a bit too sharply. He stopped dead in his tracks, almost causing me to tip the gravy boat and dish of peas and carrots that I was carrying, down the back of his Bri-nylon shirt.

We were in the little corridor between the kitchen and the guest's dining room, standing just out of sight but within earshot of the guests waiting patiently for their evening meal. With no piped music to drown out our conversation, mimed actions were the only alternative. Dad nodded to me then nodded to the roast potato languishing on the floor. Without a word spoken, I bent down, put the gravy boat on the carpet and carefully picked up the offending potato, blew on it a few times and placed it carefully back onto Dad's serving dish.

I'd been well trained.

There was no going back to Mum in the kitchen for a spare, there were no spares. She was meticulous in her food management, so much so that we very rarely got to eat what the guests had for their dinner. Many a time I'd salivate over Monday's divine smelling steak and kidney pie which were so exactly portioned out, I'm sure she used a ruler. Then there was Friday's crispy fish and chips, let alone Sunday's roast beef with all the trimmings. With homemade Apple pie and custard, a slice of Arctic roll, peach melba or ice cream with a wafer to follow.

Breakfasts would be sausage, egg and beans one day, then bacon, fried bread, egg and tinned tomato the next. With little curly pats of butter in a dish made with a butter curler, cubed sugar and a rack of toast with a pot of tea or coffee. The closest I got to eating what the guests ate was by demolishing anything left in the toast racks after their breakfasts. The curly butter pats that had gone soft though weren't for me. I liked the cold hard butter from the fridge spread in a thick layer on the cold toast. Heaven.

The main aim of anyone involved in the Summer holiday trade was to make their guests think everything was under control and they were going to have a lovely holiday without any drama or worry. When, in reality, the unexpected always seemed to rear its head behind the scenes, to which they were oblivious and caused the rest of us no end of panic and sleepless nights.

If Dad had forgotten to top up the Aga with phurnacite at lunchtime, which he kept alight in Summer to heat the water, as well as for cooking, the ovens wouldn't be hot enough to cook the dinner and the top hotplates would take ages to boil the veg. With dinner time fast approaching, panic would set, in that the meal wouldn't be ready on time and Mum wouldn't half give him what for. A couple of times they had to tell guests dinner would be late that evening.

An electric oven was bought as back up, primarily to be used in emergencies but usually, there would be simmering pots and pans and ovens utilized on both, so the kitchen would be sweltering.

The dual aspect sash windows either side would be opened to get a through draft which would then let the flies, wasps, or bees in together with the smell of manure from the stables behind the house. You couldn't win.

When the Summer Season started, all depended on when Easter fell each year, as it can fall anywhere between March 22nd and April 25th. If it was early, then the more likely that the lull in-between Easter and the real season kicking off would be longer. But generally, come March, the town would take a big yawn out of its Winter slumber and start to wake up.

Surfers would return from their winter in Biarritz. Guest houses and hotels would get painted, gardens spruced up, shops that had been closed during the Winter would get cleaned. Window displays replenished. Windbreakers, buckets and spades and postcard stands would be on show outside as the first signs of life would begin to appear. It was as if Summer's fairy dust had been sprinkled over the town, making everything pristine.

The Killacourt and Trenance Gardens would look immaculate with precision flower beds coming into bloom. Hotels would start to take on staff and a smattering of new faces would begin to appear around town as well as old familiar locals you hadn't seen all Winter. There was a tangible buzz about the town, an excitement, an expectation of good things to come.

For most, a good season would be a full six months from April to October. Foreign holidays weren't yet the norm, so Cornwall and Newquay in particular, with its seven plus glorious sandy beaches was a magnate for families. Easter would bring that first burst of excitement and optimism, The town would come alive for the four day weekend and would give the accommodation owners a chance to try out their new staff and facilities and make the necessary tweaks before the onslaught of high season.

Henver road was the gateway into the town and practically every house offered accommodation. Might only be one room, but that didn't matter as holidaymakers coming 'on spec' without a booking would just be thankful when they spotted a 'Vacancies' sign, especially in high season.

Driving down Henver road, visitors must have wondered where the sea was, if they'd driven in from Quintrell Downs direction. There was hardly a glimpse of it until past Lusty Glaze road on the right, which led to the Savoia hotel. Past the Astor cinema and King Mark on the left and then only coming down past the row of old established imposing hotels, on Narrowcliff did they get their first good view of the stunning blue of the Atlantic ocean on the horizon across the Barrowfields.

Treninnick House was a guest house when we moved in, so we'd carried on where Mrs Hook the previous owner had left off. I was still at school and helping them of an evening and weekend was a way of earning pocket money. My main job of an evening was as the washer upper. Mum would get infuriated when she'd put a pot or utensil down for a minute on the massive square kitchen table with its vinyl tablecloth.

When she turned back to pick it up, I'd have washed it.

'I've not done with that,' she'd say, annoyed. So as not to keep fighting, we came up with a rule that one side of the table, that dominated the kitchen, was hers and anything left on my side, I could wash. Beside the sink was a board hanging on the wall that she'd got in one of her auctions lots at John Julians. Really old, it had a list of food items down the left side and sliders that you could slide along to days of the week, so you'd know when you needed to buy the items.

She tried using it, but kept forgetting to look at it, before she and Dad went to Chaffins Cash and Carry up Quarry Park road, for the weekly shop. It ended up as an ornament gathering dust. I'd never seen another one like it until I spotted the exact same one on the wall of the kitchen in the Downton Abbey TV series one Sunday night.

We could take up to twelve guests depending if the family rooms were fully utilised. The four guest bedrooms were upstairs. Cliff also had his own little single room at the top of the stairs, which was so small, not viable to let out and anyway it was supposed to be haunted.

He'd bought a house up Clevedon road for him and Ushi, his German girlfriend to live in, but after they broke up he rented it out, so he was still living at home. But that proved to be a bit of a challenge because Cliff talked in his sleep and not just a mumble, he'd have a full-blown conversation with someone and you could hear every word as clear as day.

Mum and Dad were in a room downstairs to the right of the front door as you came in, with Frances and I in the room next to them. But depending on the configuration of guests booked in, those sleeping arrangements as usual were fluid and our family could end up sleeping altogether at any given time in any given room. Each room had a sink with just the one bathroom and one separate toilet between all the guests on the first floor.

We had our own bathroom and toilet downstairs. It was Saturday to Saturday bookings only, so that day was always frantic. I'd help Mum change the beds and she'd show me how to make a housewife's corner or hospital corner as it's sometimes called. The corner of the top sheet is pulled up at an angle at the bottom of the bed, the bottom part then tucked under the mattress and the top part then tucked under that, forming a very neat, mitred corner.

She was always the one for ease of maintenance so Bri-nylon sheets, the same as Dad's shirts were the order of the day, because they dried quickly and needed no ironing. I hated those sheets. When it was cooler, we had a blanket and then a candlewick bedspread on top. If you turned over in the night, the sheets were so slippery that the whole lot would end up on the floor, and you'd wake up freezing, desperately trying to pull it all back on, getting completely tangled up in the process. Or in the Winter, she'd upgrade us to those awful Winceyette flannel sheets which were pink with a square pattern.

We had so many of them, she must have got them in a job lot somewhere.

Apart from helping my parents, which was a given, I got a Saturday job, well it was actually on a Sunday. The guest house at the top of our road, Trevithick House, owned by the Barrett family, wanted somebody to serve dinner to their guests when their waitress had her night off.

Bearing in mind I was shy, this was probably not the best career move I ever made. Petrified of making direct eye contact, I could barely speak with nerves and could only carry two plates at a time, so dinner service took forever and the whole experience was excruciating.

The dining room was long and thin with tables up one side, around the top and down the other side like a squashed together horseshoe. They took about forty guests, so by the time I'd served the last guest with soup, the first table were getting increasingly impatient for their main meal.

There was no background music, nobody ever talked, or if they did it was in a whisper, so it was deadly quiet. I think they were all willing me to just hurry up and get a move on. I stuck it out for a whole summer, despite hating every minute, but the pound a week and roast dinner thrown in, that I balanced on my lap and ate on the kitchen step, was a good incentive.

We'd still get visits from the London relatives, but had less room to accommodate them, so every October, when the season was finally over, we'd go on *our* holiday, back up to London, to visit all of them. Staying in *their* cold front bedrooms on put u ups or on the floor of *their* sitting room. Newquay schools must have been a tad depleted during that month, as many other families did the same thing.

I loved staying with Mum's sister, my Auntie Lena, and Uncle Frank. He worked at the Royal Mint but had a mate that dealt in cheap Gor-ray skirts, those distinctive pleated skirts, which became a staple in Mum's wardrobe.

While we were staying there, Mum and Dad would often go to a 'Do' at the Mason's lodge with friend George Gardner, who was a member and his wife Mary. Mum would be in a lovely strapless dress with its full bouncy skirt she'd made herself for the occasion and Dad would look smart if not a little uncomfortable in his evening suit, more used to overalls than a dickie bow.

One year, Alan, my sister Frances's future husband came with us for our annual holiday. All sleeping in the front room of Auntie Betty's terraced house, Dad's younger sister, in Walthamstow. Alan went out for a pint one night on his own and couldn't remember his way home. Frances was getting frantic, as he hadn't returned hours later. Eventually the police knocked on the door, having found him wandering the streets and worked out where Alan was staying, from what he had told them. They were extremely helpful, escorting him home in their police car. Frances gave him a right earful.

Mum loved going down Walthamstow market to buy loads of material and cottons and zips and buttons. She bought all kinds of fabrics but her love affair with Crimplene dress material was endless. She loved it because it was easy to sew, hard wearing, easy to wash, needed no ironing and kept its shape, but most of all it didn't crease, no matter what you got up to.

I hated it. It was quite heavy, boring colours and patterns, with no fluidity to it. An A line skirt, never touched your legs, just stuck out at the sides. Therefore, in the mid-1960s when I wasn't yet able to buy my own clothes, my wardrobe was a homage, with skirts, dresses, trousers, even jackets made in the stuff.

I was by now been given a little more freedom. Sunday afternoons in the Winter, I'd meet up with friends at the Arcade in Central Square, where everyone congregated, because it had a great jukebox. From there we would 'promenade' through the town, hoping to spot a particular boy or other, the subject of that month's crush.

We swung from being downright scruffy to dressing up. I migrated from wearing Mum's navy double breasted coat that was way too big for me, to dressing up in my best pink coat and black patent shoes that Mum bought me back from a holiday. They were sling back, with a half inch heel, imitation leather and a red bow, I absolutely loved those shoes. When the straps finally gave out, I used Sellotape to join them back together, and still walked into town oblivious to the fact that the Sellotape was clearly visible, but there was no way I was going to give those shoes up without a fight!

Another favourite destination was Summercourt fair that had been held for over 800 years in the last week of September. It was a yearly highlight that I'd go to with friends to scream myself stupid on the big wheel, then have a battle with candyfloss, trying not to get it all over my face.

But Summercourt was also where the best fish and chip shop was, according to Dad and we wouldn't even wait to get them home but sit in the car eating them out of newspaper sodden with vinegar and lashings of salt. They never tasted better than when you had to prize off the last few chips stuck to the print.

Our first big family event in Treninnick House was Frances and Alan Greenland's wedding in October 1965 and what an hilarious day that was.

Cornish v Cockney

'Aright, my 'ansum?' said the Cornish best man.

'Watcha cock,' said my Cockney Uncle Alf in response, taking a step back, a little unsure. He hadn't been called handsome in many a year.

So far so good. At least *they* sort of understood each other. At least for the time being.

Everything had to happen in the Spring or the Autumn for us. Getting married in the Summer was a definite no, everyone was too busy earning a crust. Mum made Frances's wedding dress and my bridesmaid dress and brother Cliff did all the catering, with help from his hotel contacts. The other bridesmaid was Leslie, the young daughter of Tom and Ann, Dad's cousin, and Mum's best friend. All their family came down from London as did loads of other family and friends. Not sure where they all slept, there were tribes of them.

Borrowed tables and trestles were set up in the large rectangular lounge In Treninnick House, which was on two levels joined by a couple of steps. Half the wedding party were on the upper level and the rest on the lower level, which made for a lot of jovial banter during the meal between the supposedly 'posh' ones up top and the 'dregs' down below.

Then there was the matter of fitting everyone in. Alan had a lot of Cornish relatives too, so it was a very tight squeeze. So much so, that one person had to sit back, while the next person then leaned forward to take a bite of food and vice versa.

To cap it all, many of Alan's family didn't drink and ours did, and then some, so that added to the ambience of the day, but all in all, a day not to be forgotten, with loads of laughs.

The group wedding photo had to be taken in the back garden, there were so many people to cram in. Communication between the two sets of relatives was at times, hilarious. Cockneys doing their best to understand broad Cornish and after a few drinks, the Cockneys slipped into rhyming slang which made it impossible for the Cornish to understand a word. Add to that, our aunt, who shall be nameless having had too many sherries, started butting into conversations, trying to make sense of it all....

'I'm a bit Brahms and Liszt,' she slurred suddenly, to no-one in particular, as she slipped sideways off her chair, almost into the lap of one of Alan's mates.

'Awright'n aree?' he said lifting her gingerly back into a sitting position.

She looked perplexed and turned the other way.

'Giss on, kent be doing with none a that Brahms and Liszt rubbish,' said the stout Cornishman next to her on the other side, having overheard the conversation.

'No, no, we're from the Big Smoke not Kent,' she managed to reply, having thrown back a glass of red, belonging to the woman opposite, pinched when she wasn't looking.

Now *he* looked perplexed as he took a large bite of the piece of wedding cake that had been plonked down in front of him.

*'Proper job. Bleddy 'ansum that is,' h*e said taking another bite.

The wedding cake had been made by a holidaymaker who was a baker that had stayed in the flats at White Sails for a few years and he and his wife had become family friends. He'd made the three-tier horseshoe cake at home in London and brought it down in boxes on the train. Dad and I had gone to pick him up at Newquay station, amazed that the cake was still intact. He then did all the piping of the multitude of little horseshoes to go on it, in Mum's kitchen in Treninnick.

'Where's the lavatory?' Alan's Mum asked.

'*Up the Apples and Pears love,*' my Auntie Kath replied. '*I think you'll find Bob Hope and a clean towel in there.*'

Thinking better of it, Alan's Mum sat back down again, saying to the lady next to her…

'*I'll go dreckly. Don't want no strange man seeing my smalls.*'

And so, it carried on.

Conversations getting misconstrued. Blank expressions of bewilderment. But despite the guests not having understood a word each other had said, half the time, everyone agreed what a fabulous day it had been!

The Summer seasons came and went, with visitors returning year after year, with more becoming family friends. Dad preferred to take only pre-booked guests and we were usually full, but if for some reason, we had a vacancy you could let the tourist information office in Morfa hall, off Cliff road know and you'd usually get it filled pretty sharpish as vacant rooms in the height of the Summer were a rarity. That sometimes proved to be a challenge. Dad was no prude, but there were limits.

'Your bags are packed, now get out. Not having that kind of goings on in this house,' Dad said. He was furious. They normally only took families or couples but having a room free and on the spur of the moment took two teenage girls in, against his better judgement, staying in my old bedroom which was next to Mum and Dads room. I was out in the caravan in the car park by then. The girls were booked in for a week.

Guests weren't given a front door key usually, but if they were going to be out beyond 11 p.m., then he'd give them a key, but he didn't really settle for the night until he knew everyone was back in safely. When these girls hadn't come in on the first night of their holiday and he knew they didn't have a key, he stayed up half the night pacing the floor, getting more and more angry. By the time they crept in through the front door at 7.a.m., he was waiting for them, together with the week's money they'd paid, and their packed bags sitting by the front door.

'Not having any of those shenanigans here, this is a respectable house,' he added, as they tried without success to say they'd lost track of time and had stayed with 'a friend'. But he wasn't having any and threw them out. Luckily, there weren't many occasions like that.

Dad would eagerly read all the comments left in 'The Visitors book' after guests had left, wanting to make sure their stay had been as enjoyable as possible. The quietness of the dining room was mentioned, so he put the radio on until he sorted out some better piped music, not too loud but enough that we could get away with a few choice words or conversations in the kitchen without the guests hearing.

'*Have you heard scratching in here Doll, it wasn't half loud last night before I came to bed,*' he said to Mum, in the middle of breakfast service one morning. He rarely called her Doris, only when he was angry or trying to make a point.

We all paused for a minute, but what with kettles boiling away, eggs frying and bacon sizzling under the grill, it wasn't very conducive for hearing anything else.

Breakfast over, the hunt was on.

Treninnick house or at least the site, is mentioned in the Domesday Book, something that Dad was proud about. Next to the kitchen and accessed by a door and then down a few steps was the 'Stockroom' as we called it and beyond that but accessed from outside was a storeroom where Dad kept the phurnacite for the Aga. That outside storeroom, together with the barn in the car park, were reputed to be the oldest parts of the property, with their cob walls.

The large internal stockroom was just that, a naturally cold room housing two large deep freezers, Mum's Twin tub washing machine, a butler sink and rows of shelving around the walls, holding flour and dried goods and tins and packets and catering sizes of every description.

'*I bet we've got mice,*' he said, opening the door and stepping down into that cold room.

Mum pulled a face and I grimaced.

Finding no evidence and nothing to show in the traps he put down, we temporarily forgot about it.

Until we all heard it again, days later, late one evening, louder than ever.

'*It's right above us,*' Dad said, looking up at the kitchen ceiling. '*Don't understand, it's a flat roof.*'

He got the stepladders out the next day and went to investigate, thinking it might just be a bird's nest or something.

'*I think we've got rats,*' he said. He'd worked on all kinds of old buildings and knew the different signs between mice and rats, so he seemed sure. '*There's a hole just by the drainpipe and the asphalt is lifted.*'

'*Well I'm not going in that stockroom,*' I said quickly, thinking that's where they'd probably find their way to next.

The rat man came, but not before we had a few sleepless nights, imagining them scurrying around.

'*It's a large nest,*' he said, coming back into the kitchen after his investigation. Mum and I shivered, not wanting to know the ins and outs of how he was going to get rid of them, just wanted them gone.

Surprisingly, that was the only episode we had of unwanted creatures that I knew about, but I was always scared in the Winter, when Mum and Dad went for a night out to the Roses Association and I was left on my own. The Roses met at the Beachcroft hotel on Cliff Road. I'm not sure how they came to join, as it was originally set up for Yorkshire and Lancashire people.

I'd sit in the 'Breakfast room' watching the television, while they were out. We assumed the room was called that because it was where the previous owner had served breakfast to her guests.

It was a room next to the kitchen that we used in the Summer as our lounge, come dining room come everything. In the winter, if Dad didn't want to light the coal fire in the big lounge, we'd watch the television in the breakfast room as it was always warm, because it was close to the Aga.

It was where we'd be sitting with Frances and Alan not long after they'd had their daughter Luci and they'd put her asleep in her carry cot on the dining table.

We'd all be watching television and suddenly, Luci would prop herself up and a little head would appear over the side of the carry cot, making us laugh, then she'd drop down and a few minutes later, her little head would appear again. She was so funny.

I didn't like being on my own in Treninnick of an evening. I loved living there, but it was old and it creaked and it made noises and there were gaps under every door and I'd be convinced of seeing small things running past the other side and if that wasn't enough it was supposed to be haunted.

My 'winter' bedroom was at the back overlooking the garden, with of course its own sink. I had a double bed and there was a single bed pushed against the opposite wall which I had to pull out to get to a cupboard recessed in the wall, where I hid my diary. The diary, where I wrote everything that happened, every day. Under that bed I kept my reel to reel tape recorder. I'd pestered Mum and Dad for ages, and I'd got it for Christmas. I'd tape the top forty hosted by Alan 'Fluff' Freeman, from my radio every Sunday teatime as it was counted down. Despite sometimes missing part of a song because the radio faded in and out, I could play my favourite songs over and over on my recorder.

If they weren't back from the Roses, by the time I went to bed, I'd bang off the lights as I went and race up the stairs, along the corridor, rush into my room at the back, slam the door, scramble into my nightdress, dive into bed and pull the covers right over my head. Out of breath, heart pumping, scared stiff!

So, still in my mid-teens, I swung from being a scaredy cat one minute, afraid of ghosts and things that go bump in the night, to thinking I was old enough to make some of my own decisions. With that in mind, having saved up pocket money, I bought my first pair of Levi jeans without telling or rather asking Mum first.

Bad mistake.

They were all the rage, and I was determined to buy a pair, so had saved up the four pounds needed and nervously walked into His Casuals on Station parade. It was only a small shop with the counter suspended by two chains hanging from the ceiling and it was one of the Parkin brothers behind the counter. Levi's only made men's jeans so I tried a few pairs on before I found a small enough pair for me and thrilled with my purchase, skipped home.

'Girls don't wear denim. Denim is for men, you can't wear those, take them back,' was all Mum said. End of conversation. He was very understanding when I returned them, stumbling my way through an excuse as to why I needed a refund. Embarrassed. Again.

No, it was still crimplene for me, even when I went on my one and only school trip.

Pass the sick bucket

'You look like a foreign orchestra coming down the gangplank,' Mum said, laughing, as Dad picked up my case and we headed off to the car.

The only time I ever had a proper holiday during the Summer, was when I was fifteen and went on my one and only school trip. A cruise to the Baltic, visiting Finland, Norway, Denmark, and Russia. All my pals were going as well as my best friend Charmaine Stoneman. I hadn't always been friends with her, but we got to talking one day, as I'd often see her pass our house to visit her Gran and Grandad, Mr and Mrs Wilton who lived in a cottage at the back, just past the stables in Treninnick.

We soon realised that we both had a mutual love of dancing and music and the beach and of course surfing, well not actually surfing, more like surfers. She was a black haired Twiggy. Same slim figure, same pigeon-toed stance and whatever she wore looked great on her. We were so excited to be going on this trip. There was a direct coach from Newquay to Plymouth every Saturday, so Char (pronounced Shar) as I called her and I took the trip on our own one week, to buy some clothes. I wanted at least one dress to take with me that wasn't crimplene.

My brother Cliff had given me some money, bless him, and I'd saved my pocket money so off we went. I bought a bright yellow scooped neck button down shirt dress with pockets in the front and a real leather beige Safari bag which had loads of pockets. I loved that bag. Mum bought me a new suitcase and she had my initials, DJB, for Denise June Bullen, put on the side.

Not sure if that was because she thought someone might steal it, which was highly unlikely as it was a horrible shade of brown or if I'd mislay it and they'd easily know who it belonged to. Over fifty years on and many house-moves later, I've still got that suitcase up in the loft gathering dust and looking sorry for itself, but can't seem to part with it, purely for nostalgic reasons, you understand.

We had to wear our school uniform at various times throughout the trip, but mandatory on the day we caught the train at Truro taking us to Falmouth to embark the ship. Poor Leslie Mather had done something to her arm and found it difficult keeping her blazer thrown over her sling, which she had to keep on for the whole trip. We managed to ditch the hats, thank goodness and were able to wear our own clothes at other times, but when seen to be representing the school, wearing the uniform was a given.

There were several different schools from all over Cornwall, so lots of new people to eye up, boys to fancy, new friends to make and ship to explore. We slept in dormitories crammed with bunk beds. I was assigned a top bunk with Char underneath. Our cases were stored below the bottom bunk and each had a small cupboard for our clothes. On the first day, the excitement was palpable, all was going swimmingly, the sea was calm, the weather fine, the canteen was full, deck games were being played and everyone began to relax.

Then we reached the North Sea and all hell broke loose.

Bad weather suddenly hit the ship and the swell knocked us all for six. The seasickness came across the whole ship in waves, affecting some of us, leaving others alone, temporarily. Then just when you thought it had passed you by and you'd found your sea legs and were okay, it suddenly hit and you'd have to rush to the side or to the toilet, whichever was nearest.

Everybody was grey, listless, and confined to their bunk beds where teachers and the ship's staff hovered with wet flannels and sick buckets. Most of my friends had succumbed but I was fine until I went into the almost empty canteen for lunch and was transfixed by the view out of the porthole across the room which was filled one minute with sky and the next with sea as the swell was that fierce. So, I didn't escape, I don't think anybody did. It was the sour smell of sick all over the place combined with the unwelcome food smells wafting up from the canteen that made the nausea even worse. Plus, the moans and groans from those bed-ridden in close proximity all around you, made for a very uncomfortable twenty-four hours.

After that day of hell, the sea calmed, the sun came out and people slowly emerged from the gloom of the dormitories onto the warm decks, getting their sea legs and the trip began in real earnest. There were a lot of planned games and activities, talks and films to watch. But we liked to hang out by the small swimming pool, which we took full advantage of. While others just looked on afraid to show themselves in swimsuits or get their hair wet, we didn't care and had every intention of trying everything on board.

We met a chap called Gary, an American who liked hanging around with us. He had a broken foot, so our little crew made a strange sight, what with his foot and Leslie's arm both in plaster.

Mum had made me a sleeveless dress to wear over my swimsuit in the dreaded Crimplene. Everyone else was in cool cotton tops that fluttered in the breeze. I sweltered in the dense unforgiving fabric.

We visited Copenhagen, such a clean city with its famous little mermaid statue on the waterfront and had a great night at Tivoli Gardens. Then Helsinki, having a tour of the 1952 Olympic stadium, stopping off at a lovely peaceful island off Norway before dropping anchor at Leningrad, Russia, now known as St. Petersburg, the highlight of the trip.

When we arrived at the docks in Russia, it was like entering another time zone. There were traditional dancers to greet us on the docks while soldiers with guns hovered close by. We were given a good talking to, by our teachers and told that we should in no circumstances ever attempt to walk through the docks on our own if we got lost, as security was extreme and it was too dangerous.

Some of the kids were going further on into Moscow for a day, but that was more expensive and Mum and Dad couldn't stretch to that at the time, but to be honest Leningrad was captivating and was enough for me to take in, otherwise I would have had culture overload.

The highlights were a night at the Russian ballet which was mesmerising and a visit to the Winter Palace. The splendour, opulence, the richness of colour and priceless treasures was staggering. As we were driving through the streets, the overriding sight though, was of soldiers everywhere, wielding those Kalashnikovs. It was unnerving.

The Palace itself, now part of the Hermitage museum, was grey on the outside masking the great treasures held within and it was easy to understand why there was the uprising against the Tsar back in 1917, when the people were starving in the streets and all this wealth was owned by the royal household. I was in awe as we walked from room to room and an experience I will never forget.

The gardens of the palace were immaculate but again patrolled by a battalion of armed soldiers and I must admit it did put the fear of God into us and we were glad to get back to the safety of the ship. But that wasn't before we visited some shops to get souvenirs. I came away with a Babushka doll, a traditional wooden nesting set of five dolls, one inside the other, which I still have.

However, the main souvenir of choice, for everyone it seemed, including me, was the Balalaika, a triangle shaped stringed instrument that had been given a starring role in Dr Zhivago, a film from the previous year. They must have been cheap, because the sight of hundreds of kids getting off the ship in Falmouth, with one of those slung over their shoulder, on our homecoming must have been hilarious to our families waiting on the dock.

I haven't got a musical bone in my body, for playing an instrument that is, so what possessed me to buy it I don't know. Must have been caught up in the moment.

Mine was soon despatched to the loft having been produced and shown to every disinterested relative or friend that happened to visit and I kept it for years.

Despite there being lots of new people to meet, we preferred hanging around with the lads from our class. We knew them well, could have a good laugh and felt comfortable in their company.

I bet there's still a few of them got their Balalaikas, stashed away and forgotten in lofts. Reminders of a great time we all had on that cruise.

Sand, sea and surfers

'He likes girls with a bit of meat on them,' Mrs Wilson said.

My hopes were dashed. I couldn't have made it more obvious that I fancied Robin, her son. But with me, not having an ounce of spare flesh on show in my bikini, that comment was devastating. Char and I would go down to the Great Western Beach most days in summer, even if the sun wasn't cracking the flags, we'd be there, just to hang around with the surfers. Hang around is a slight exaggeration when they hardly gave us a second glance, but just to be on the same beach, in the same vicinity was enough.

'Newquay 3564,' I answered, having rushed to the phone, before Dad got there.

'Den, it's me, Char, are you going down?'

'Yeah, I'll see you by the monument at 12.'

We'd always meet by the granite Tolcarne Cross monument at the bottom of Edgcumbe Avenue. She would come from her house in Hillgrove Road and if she was a bit late, I'd read the inscription on the monument *'Restored Sir Robert Edgecumbe'* for the umpteenth time or watch the leisurely game of bowls going on just behind it, to pass the time.

Even in school holidays we had to help our respective parents with household chores before we could go out and have some fun. Her parents lived in a bungalow but let out the one spare room for bed and breakfast and my Mum and Dad were now running Treninnick House as a B&B, so I'd help Mum out by making beds, or washing up or just being a general dogsbody.

After my chores, I wouldn't waste precious sun-bathing time by having lunch at home, so I'd normally buy a steak and kidney pie from the kiosk at the bottom of the hill on the beach. Or I'd quickly make up a salad in a plastic container with anything I could find in our fridge. Lettuce, radish, tomatoes, ham or cheese and even baked beans would get tossed in if they were going.

Sunscreen wasn't the thing, wasn't on the agenda, wasn't talked about. What was talked about was how to achieve the quickest, deepest tan possible. The 'suntan lotion' of choice was either oil and vinegar mixed, with which you'd fry and stink to high heaven or coconut oil.

This came in a jar from Boots and would be white and solid when you bought it and then as soon as it was left out in the sun for a bit, would start to melt and become clear. Both oily and messy, giving no protection whatever from the harmful UV rays, which was something that wasn't recognised as an issue. Not realising the damage it was doing to our skin, but boy did it get you brown!

The Great Western was just one of the seven plus glorious beaches around Newquay, but it was the nearest to where we both lived and luckily was *the* beach of choice for the surfers. The entrance to it, sandwiched between the Blue Lagoon on the left and the Great Western Hotel on the right. The incredibly steep hill down to the beach, known as 'The Slope', was where you'd have to hold on to the wall to stop you breaking into a run. Always a bracing wind at the top, but the panoramic view of the dramatic coastline was spectacular. Against the backdrop of towering, rugged cliffs, you can see right across Newquay Bay, past Towan Beach to the Harbour and up to the majestic Atlantic Hotel perched on top of the hill, far in the distance.

Halfway down the 'the slope' was a platform containing benches for those that couldn't quite make it the whole way down or needed a rest on the arduous climb back up. A great vantage point, to watch the surfers, even in the Winter, when they'd brave the weather in wetsuits.

Every day, we'd eagerly anticipate that this would be the day when one of the surfers would notice us, let alone talk to us, with Chris Jones, Robin Wilson and Roger Mansfield being the young surfers of the moment. Roger's family owned the Penthouse restaurant on Cliff road, now called the Griffin. He was the talk of our class at Grammar school, because he wore white socks with his school uniform.

We'd spread our towels out on the sand, just at the bottom of the hill to be as near as possible to them, as they congregated by the entrance, leaning their surfboards up against the cliffs. We'd watch them lovingly wax their surfboards, which helped with the grip, apparently, when catching waves. They'd spend ages doing it, making us wonder if they gave such careful attentive consideration to their girlfriends, as they showed to those surfboards. We lived in hope that they did.

We got to know other local beach goers, one of whom was a very chatty lady who was always down there with younger children and we found out after a while that this was Robin Wilson's Mum. Well, we thought we'd cracked it, so we'd position ourselves as close to her little group as possible and it soon started paying off. Robin and his friends would come over to get food or a drink or just have a chat with his Mum and we soon got embroiled in the conversations. We'd be thrilled.

They all wore Bermuda shorts and so did we, except theirs were authentic, bright, and colourful, the real McCoy and ours were home-made. I was determined that when I could afford it, I'd be buying a pair from the Maui surf shop at the top of the hill, next to the entrance to the Blue Lagoon.

We'd be on the beach every day whatever the weather, having to huddle under our towels sometimes from a passing shower. Only torrential rain kept us away.

That Summer saw the Great Western Beach host the surf championships, on a rare, overcast, miserable day where the damp mist frizzed up your hair. Char and I had positioned ourselves just along from the entrance, backs against the cold rocks, freezing, thinking we must be mad not to be home in the dry. I'd brought a flask of soup down to warm us up, as nothing was going to deter us from being amongst the elite surfers.

I finally saved up enough to buy a proper pair of Bermudas. They were vivid orange and white swirls, with a thick white drawstring at the waist and white cuffs at the bottom. Cut beautifully, so flattering despite them being men's sizes yet again. I loved those shorts. Mum had to drag them off me to be washed, but the beauty of them was that they dried in a flash. They were the only pair of *real* Bermuda shorts I ever had. Mum used to make mine and I made myself a black pair edged with a row of purple bias binding that drew loads of comments. Even from strangers....

'Give us a lick of your ice cream,' he said.

I was walking past Menzies on Bank street with Judith, a girl I knew from around town. She was always tapping me up for money to buy a Vesta curry and rice for her lunch and we were on our way to her house at the top of St. Georges road for her to cook it, where she wouldn't offer me so much as a bite.

'Go on, give us a lick,' he said again, which I duly did, holding the Cornish ice cream cornetto towards him. He was slim, had gorgeous smiley eyes, dark hair, and an accent I couldn't quite place. He and two mates had been standing talking as we passed by and as they moved off, he turned back and shouted,

'Love the shorts.'

That Summer seemed endless. I hadn't realised how treasured those memories were until I read a book by Emma Smith called 'The Great Western Beach' which relates to her own childhood, centred around the same beach but some thirty years previous. Little had changed.

The beach in her time had not been commercialised in any way. In her day Stefani's Ice cream van came right down onto the beach for refreshment. Families would take down picnics just like we had done, and her description of those times brought it all back, clear and vivid. How innocent and vulnerable

Char and I were, but how excited also at the prospect of boys and going on dates and all that palaver.

I wrote to Emma Smith in 2009, saying how much I had enjoyed her book, explaining that I knew some of the families, or their descendants and worked in some of the hotels she mentioned. I received a lovely letter back from her telling me that she had made one or two awful bloomers, due to misinformation she had been given, but soon rectified them with the families concerned.

I worry sometimes that everything I am telling you in this book, did happen, or did I dream some of it up or been misinformed? Only time will tell. What I didn't make up was Mrs Wilson's comments about her son Robin's preferences when it came to girlfriends.

Consequently, by the end of that Summer, Robin Wilson had been dumped in my affections and my attention had firmly moved on to Chris Jones, who without realising it, had given me a smidgeon of encouragement, just before we'd gone on holiday at the end of that Summer.

'Wake up dear, wake up, it's late.'

Mum was shaking me.

I slowly emerged from under the covers. I didn't know what a duvet was, let alone sleep under one until we went on that holiday to Switzerland. I was more used to that Bri-nylon sheet, blanket, candlewick bedspread combination, which frustratingly kept slipping onto the floor. No such problem this night though. I'd been all toasty and snug, cocooned beneath a super warm, luxuriously deep duvet that never moved all night. No wonder I'd slept in.

'You've missed breakfast,' she said
That soon woke me up. I loved my food.

We were staying in a hotel right by Lake Lucerne in Switzerland. It was the one and only foreign adventure we ever had as a family and only the second and last time we ever stayed in a hotel together. Ironic really when you think how involved we were ourselves in the tourist trade. But our holidays usually consisted of sleeping on a rickety old camp bed in Auntie Lena's icy cold front bedroom in Loughton, Essex, on our annual Autumn trip back to London to visit relatives. Therefore, sleeping under the warmth of this luxurious duvet in an actual bed, was a real treat.

We were on an all-inclusive coach trip, taking us from Cornwall to Dover and then the ferry across to France, staying in Reims for our first night stopover with a quick look around Reims cathedral the next morning.

Famous as the place where thirty-three French kings were crowned.

Then on to Epernay for a tour of Moet and Chandon the famous champagne makers, seeing the labyrinthine of cellars, followed by a tasting. I was told it was divine, but I never did become a champagne drinker, too many bubbles up your nose for my liking.

On to Lucerne, a stunning city with medieval architecture and spectacular lake views. Immaculate spotless streets to wander down, as we browsed the exclusive expensive shop windows, feeling refreshed by the crisp, clean air coming down from the mountains.

Along with me, Mum, Dad, Cliff, Frances, and her husband Alan, on this trip were Jack Phillips, the butcher from Cubert, his wife Connie and their son Peter, who I'd had a crush on for ages, so I was really looking forward to spending some quality time in close proximity to him.

It was October, the only time we could take our holidays. No penalties back then for taking your child out of school during term time. I just had to catch up when I got back. It didn't seem to do me any harm. It should have been snowing in Switzerland, a proper Winter Wonderland, but I hate the cold, so thankfully it was lovely weather with misty mornings dawning across the lake and bright sunny days.

We'd go to a bar by the hotel of an evening and I'd be fascinated by the mammoth glasses of beer that the waitresses were handing out. Gripping two in each hand, foaming beer sloshing everywhere as they were carried from bar to table.

Our group soon got talking to the locals who could speak good English and we had a fun time. I wore a bought dress for a change, no home-made crimplene in sight. It was a green floral halter neck empire line and Mum let me wear her white imitation furry jacket over the top as my arms were bare and it was a bit chilly, when the sun went down.

The day before we were going on this holiday, I'd gone into Newquay to get a few last-minute toiletries from Boots on Bank street. Then as it was a lovely October day, chilly but sunny, I walked the long way home.

Along Cliff road, up Narrowcliff, turning down Ulalia road, by the side of the Bristol hotel. Where, who do I spot washing a snazzy sports car at the back of the Bella Vista hotel but…. Chris Jones.

He shouted hi, smiled, and waved, water spraying everywhere from the foamy sponge in his hand. I was dumbstruck as per usual, couldn't utter a word. Just about managed a smile, before walking on, heart pounding, knowing that this brief encounter was all the encouragement I'd needed to make him my next focus of attention.

From Lucerne, we visited Interlaken and Grindelwald, staying in traditional chalets ending up in Wengen, with views overlooking a spectacular waterfall. With the slopes being snow free, we'd take the hiking paths in the warm sunshine, fascinated by the huge bells around the necks of the cows grazing on the hillsides. They have them on so the farmers can keep track of them when they are out of view on the hilly landscape.

The highlight of the trip had to be the trip on the wooden train up to the highest station in Europe on the Jungfrau mountain. The snow deep and glistening, the air crisp and clear and sunlight so bright, too bright without sunglasses and the panoramic scenery from the viewing stage incredible. It was like being on the top of the World.

All too soon it was home time and as everyone got off the coach in Newquay with large cow bells of various sizes, as souvenirs, it looked like we'd just come back from a bell ringing convention.

Yes, 1966 had been an eventful year.

It had been our first full year of running a guest house. I'd been on that school cruise in June. Dad had set up a television in the guest's lounge so they could watch England win the World Cup, triumphantly lifting the trophy in the July. Frances had left Beresford Motors after getting married and she and Alan had opened the Fruit Basket up Fore street, selling fruit and veg, where I helped them out sometimes, for extra pocket money.

I was allowed a bit more freedom to go to youth clubs and friend's houses and parties and it was after that trip to Switzerland that Mum was first diagnosed with Brucellosis.

Blue Lagoon – Take 2

'Well you're not wearing that,' Mum said as I came into the kitchen. I was wearing a black jumper she'd knitted me with lacy sleeves.

Although I was still skinny, I was starting to fill out and it clung in all the right places or wrong places, depending on whose perspective it was. She made me put another white jumper underneath and to be fair it looked quite effective with the white showing through the lacy arms.

I was finally being allowed out to my first ever dance at the St. Brannocks hotel, which had a Big Beat Dance every Friday. Of course, it was on the understanding that Dad would drop me off right outside and come to pick me up again afterwards. The more I danced that night the hotter I got in the two sweaters, until eventually I had to go outside before I collapsed with the heat.

Mum was a great seamstress, and I did like a lot of the clothes that she made me. It was just the crimplene I couldn't stand. The silky deep purple mini tent dress with white spots was a favourite, which I wore for the first time a few weeks later.

'Ahhh, you can see your underwear,' Char said laughing, pointing at me as we boogied on down to Martha and the Vandellas blasting out Jimmy Mack.

'Haha, I can see yours, and your teeth are glowing,' I said pointing back.

It was courtesy of the fluorescent lighting over the small dancefloor of the upstairs disco of the King Mark on Narrowcliff, which showed gleaming white bra and knickers through your clothes and made your teeth look luminous. I shouldn't have been, but I was thrilled at the attention that brought.

It was on that night that I got my first glimpse of a group of lads that were all smartly suited and booted and the most fantastic dancers. Didn't need a partner, just took to the dance floor on their own or with each other and stunned us with their rhythm and moves, energy and enthusiasm. We couldn't help but stand back and let them take over to the Motown sounds blasting out.

We knew they weren't local by their accents and when we started to see them around town, realised they must be hotel workers. I didn't anticipate then what an impact they were going to have on my life.

Not sure if it was Bill Hibbert that had the King Mark at that time, but he certainly did a few years later, a well-known Newquay face.

It was for my sixteenth birthday that summer, that my parents had finally relented and allowed me to go to the Blue Lagoon for the Saturday night dance. I had on hipster trousers with that same black lacy jumper without the second jumper underneath this time and a white belt doing its best to keep the jumper tucked in. I had imitation drop pearl earrings that screwed onto my earlobes, which I loved and kept for years.

I'd expected it to be the same as my ballroom dancing days. But gone were the palm tree pillars, which, when it was redeveloped in the mid-1960s, were taken away before the builders realised they actually were holding up the ceiling, which I believe contributed to half of the roof collapsing.

Gone were the large murals of all those scantily dressed beauties and gone was the drab and dim, unlit dance floor I remembered. There was a bar on the upper level facing the sea, reached by stairs either end, the stage was brightly lit, with subdued lighting over the huge dancefloor which would get packed.

This became our go to venue most Saturday nights from then on. I went there so often that even if my friends weren't going, I would venture there on my own. Which was a bit of a breakthrough in the confidence stakes. But that was only because I was sure of bumping into somebody I knew. I just wanted to dance.

I was fine when it came to talking to friends and people I knew well. It was talking to strangers that always got me in a tizzy, never knowing what to say. As for flirting, well that was never a skill I got the hang of. I was and always have been a great listener, very interested in what other people had to say. Quite content to stay in the background as I usually found other people's conversations and lives much more fascinating than anything I had to say.

But bumping into a girl who was dressed in a frock like mine was not on the agenda, when I'd gone on my own one night. Her Mum had obviously bought the same purple polka dot material, probably from Hawke and Thomas on Bank street and made her a dress almost identical. We looked like the terrible twins, trying to avoid each other all night.

There was always live music, some local groups like the **Vigilantes and the Fenmen, but then other more famous ones like the Applejacks, Screaming Lord Sutch, Wishful thinking and The Merseys. But my absolute all-time favourites were** Geno Washington and the Ram Jam band. Geno, born William Francis Washington in 1943, in Indiana, was electrifying on stage and I'd be there right at the front doing my funky chicken or a good imitation at least.

My Dad would always arrange to pick me up and drop Char off home as well and then sometimes her Dad would do the same for me. However, after a while we'd tell each other's Dads that it was the other's turn that week to give ourselves a bit of freedom and on one such night, I got talking to another of the Parkin brothers. There were four brothers that I know of, Ian, Robin, Andy and Chris. Whichever it was, offered to walk me home not realising how far it was and everything was going fine until we got to the viaduct and I told him there was another mile or so to go, up the steep hill to Treninnick. His smile faded.

If you weren't used to climbing that hill, it could be daunting and I felt sorry for him, so I gave him a quick kiss and said I'd be fine on my own from there. I'd often end up doing that walk alone when boys realised where I lived but it didn't upset me. I just got used to it.

Everyone would congregate in the Great Western Bar before going across to the Blue. It was nowhere near as big as it is now, it was just the front part, with the bar on the right side as you went in with tables and seats to the left. It got packed, with only one way in and out. I'd try to mingle with the crowd before getting spotted as being underage and shown the door.

I always seemed to be on the outside looking in. Too young to be drinking, so the Great Western and the Sailors were out of bounds legally and even the Toddle Inn, up Fore street, that *'den of iniquity,'* as my mother called it, was a slightly older generation, only a year or two, but enough to make me still feel like a kid. I did try my first and last cigarette outside the Toddle though. Someone gave me a go and I nearly choked. Thankfully, that put paid to me ever wanting to try them again.

The Tall Trees club with live bands and the Wigwam club in the basement with cabaret artists and comedians was another popular venue, on Tolcarne road, behind the Grammar school. It was where my siblings and many of the hotel workers went for a night out. But my friends stuck to the Blue and I loved it.

It's a miracle I ever managed to get through my early teenage years, unharmed, unscathed, and intact. I wonder if I was naïve or just plain dumb! I got myself into a few sticky situations.

Too young to be drinking and I looked it. I didn't have any of that bravado that some other girls of my age seemed to have that saw them get away with all kinds. The worst I did was walk slowly through the 'Roof Top' bar, in the Blue, trying to spot boys I fancied or I'd have to race through, because I'd been spotted by the barman or the manager. Making my escape by the other set of stairs at the far end.

'Do you do it?' this older lad said that I knew from around town.

'Do what?' I replied, as I loitered on the stairs at the far end of the bar.

'You know….it.'

I didn't have a clue what he was talking about.

'Yes, I think I do, yes I'm sure I do, yes,' I said bravely, not realizing what I was admitting to. He laughed and went on his way.

You could get a pass out, for a bit of fresh air and to make sure you could get back in again. One time I went outside with a boy I'd only just met. He wasn't a local. We walked down the steep hill onto the Great Western Beach in the pitch black. I was just out for a kiss and cuddle and that was going fine until he had other ideas. He must have realised he'd picked a dud, so pulled me up from the damp sand and walked me back up the hill to the dance. I never saw him again. If he had been a less than savoury character, things could have been different, but I was so trusting, it hadn't dawned on me that something nasty could have happened.

Starting to get a bit wiser as time wore on, I took less chances with boys I didn't know and went out more often with local lads. But that proved my undoing one eventful Saturday night….

'Get out the car, now,' Dad yelled as he pulled open the door and grabbed my arm. I got a shock, I hadn't seen him come out the gate, but I knew he'd be angry, it was well past my curfew. Chris disentangled himself from me as Dad yanked me out the seat.

'In, now,' he added as he marched through the gate to our front door, me trailing behind. I didn't even get a chance to say goodnight before I was dragged away from the one person, I'd waited so long to even notice me, let alone be snogging on the front seat of his car. I was beside myself.

Dad was already back in bed, by the time I stormed into their bedroom. I had no idea what time it was.

'How could you do that to me, that was humiliating, he was only giving me a lift home, he'll never speak to me again,' I yelled through snotty tears.

'He was doing more than giving you a lift home, from what I could see,' Dad said

'It was just a goodnight kiss,' I tried to argue, knowing full well, it was a bit more than that.

It was Mum's turn to try and broker some peace, but Dad wasn't having any. He turned away, switched off his bedside lamp and lay down.

End of conversation.

I'd fancied Chris Jones, my innocent co-conspirator, for ages, ever since he passed me outside my classroom at Newquay Grammar, smiled and said hello. He looked back at me, I looked back at him, well that was it. From that moment, seeing his sun-bleached blond hair tickling his collar and that dazzling smile, I was smitten. He was the junior surfing champion of Great Britain and I'd watch him for hours, surf the waves on Great Western Beach. But I thought I had no chance until he waved at me that time at the back of the Bella Vista hotel. I didn't need much encouragement. At least he hadn't said he liked girls with a bit more meat on them like Robin Wilson had. At least not to my knowledge.

I'd been at the Blue Lagoon that Saturday night as usual, but I'd been going out with Neil Mason, Chris's friend, for a while. Neil also went to Newquay Grammar, drove a car and was a nice enough lad. We'd go to White Cross sometimes because they had a disco.

Neil would pick me up and get me back well before my curfew of 10.30. But whenever we went to 'The Blue', he always said he'd meet me inside, which started to annoy me and I couldn't understand why he wouldn't meet me outside, like a proper date. I began to feel he didn't want his mates to see he was dating, either that or he didn't want to pay my entrance fee.

Anyway, I'd had enough that night and finished with him after a few dances and went to join some friends on the dancefloor. The band went off to take a break and I was sitting on the edge of the stage, when next minute, Chris Jones comes up to me and starts chatting, asking me why I'd finished with Neil. When I explained, he asked me if I'd re-consider and I said no, I'd had enough. He was very charming and concerned and asked me if I wanted a lift home as Neil obviously wouldn't be doing that now.

I jumped at the chance.

It was only when we got outside that he told me that his mini was back at his house, so we'd need to walk there first to pick it up. Didn't realise that he lived on Headland Road at the time, up by Fistral Beach, in the complete opposite direction to where I should be going home, to Treninnick. A long, long walk.

I didn't care.

I was just ecstatic that here I was walking through Newquay with the boy of my dreams. At last. He was a proper gentleman and made sure that he was always walking on the roadside of the pavement. He made a point of it, which has always stuck with me, because not many boys that I went out with did that. We chatted away and I knew I was going to be incredibly late getting home but wasn't bothered and when he held my hand, I thought, yes, I've cracked it, I was going to be his girlfriend.

Or so I thought. But Dad scuppered that before it even got started, so that one evening proved to be our one and only semi-romantic encounter. He was a year or two older than me. Old enough to drink and I wasn't, so that didn't help. I'd bump into him now and again, more often when Dad turned our guest house into a Pub, a few years later. Chris would come in for a drink with his girlfriend at the time and I often wondered if he realised where he was, who the landlord was and if he was just a tad worried that he might be thrown out at any minute, for that past misdemeanour.

So, 1967 had been another eventful year. The Torrey Canyon had run aground in the March, depositing crude oil in many of Cornwall's magnificent beaches. My brother Cliff went down to Holywell to help clear it up.

Saturday night dancing had become a regular thing for me and Char. If we weren't at the 'Blue', we'd go to the dance up at the Pentire Hotel and be transfixed watching a lad called Pablo take over the floor with his moves. I could have watched him all night. I'd been on proper dates. Had proper boyfriends, not just boys that were friends.

Then, just as the frenzy of the high Summer season was long gone and we were starting to get our Newquay back, that more sedate, relaxed, calm place to be, the biggest band in history descended on the town. I'd just started my A level year that September, when the Beatles, my teenage idols, who I'd thought I would adore forever, visited the town as part of their Magical Mystery tour filming. Staying at the Atlantic Hotel, they attracted fans, hotel workers, locals, all desperate to get near and have photos taken with them.

Where was I? Well my adoration for them had ebbed and I couldn't be bothered walking up to the Atlantic after school and then walking all the way back home to Treninnick, so I didn't go.

One of my biggest regrets.

At sixteen, I was still naïve, still ridiculously shy at times, still a teenage schoolgirl, not having an inkling of the next massive change that was to come my way that Christmas. I had no idea what was in store, or the topsy turvy impact it would have on my life. 1967 was to be my last year of schoolgirl innocence.

Mind the stairs

'Quick, in the kitchen,' Mrs Boxer said, pushing me down the corridor. But not before I'd spotted the coffin being precariously manhandled down the front stairs of the Minerva hotel, by two men in black suits. A third was standing at the bottom whispering instructions.

'Come on lads, quick as you can and mind the stairs.'

However, his attempt at keeping a bit of decorum in the proceedings was suddenly thwarted when the man at the top missed his footing as they manoeuvred around the half landing and the coffin suddenly lurched, banging against the wall, then as he tried to regain control, his elbow knocked the already loose ornamental wooden ball off the top of the bannister, which proceeded to bounce down every remaining step, making a hell of a racket. Mrs B was beside herself, as I entered the kitchen.

I could still hear her firing instructions to the undertakers as she choreographed the quick exit of the deceased, out to the waiting black van, before any more mishaps and the other guests awoke. It was 6.45 a.m.

Mary and Kathy, the other two chambermaids, both from southern Ireland, were already sitting at the kitchen table. Mary, five foot nothing, buxom, with glorious shiny black bobbed hair, and thick, black rimmed glasses, was sitting quietly sipping her tea.

Nothing seemed to faze her. She was the voice of reason and my 'go to' for any advice if I wasn't sure how to do something. Kathy on the other hand, was a nervous wreck, frantically puffing away on a cigarette, smoke billowing everywhere, despite the bacon and eggs being prepared for the guest's breakfast.

Tall, sturdily built with broad shoulders, she seemed quite intimidating at first, someone who you wouldn't want to pick a fight with, but in fact was really a total softy who took everything to heart. She was talking twenty to the dozen as usual. When she was in full swing, her Irish lilt made it impossible for me to understand a word, so Mary had to translate for me. Kathy was without doubt a glass half empty kind of girl, whose life was governed by omens, fate, and foreboding, but she did make me laugh and I'd warmed to them both straightaway. I'd only been a hotel chambermaid for a month, but I felt at home already.

The Minerva, like many of the hotels, had opened at Easter, the official start of the Summer Season in Newquay. Mary and Kathy had started several weeks before, to spring clean all the rooms and I started a couple of days before the first guests arrived, just to familiarise myself with the routine and layout of the hotel, which was a bit higgledy piggledy and took me a while to get used to.

I was so nervous on my first day. I'd helped Mum lots of times in the guest house, making beds, cleaning sinks, but I'd never worked in a proper hotel, so didn't know what to expect.

I was fearful of becoming Cinderella to two ugly sisters and given all the horrible jobs to do. But that couldn't have been further from the truth.

There was always a bit of a false start to the season with a few days of frenzy over the Easter weekend when the town would come to life after the long Winter and holidaymakers would once again amble down the main street or venture down the beach if the weather allowed, depending on whether Easter was early or late. But then after that initial burst of activity, the town went quiet again before the Summer really got going, when factories up country would shut down for their break or it was the school holidays. So, the hotels filled that intervening gap with coach parties, allowing staff to be kept on throughout and for the momentum of the summer season to be maintained.

These out of season trips in Spring and Autumn were particularly popular with the elderly, as transport, accommodation, food, and day trips were all included, so great value. You could tell what time of year it was by the volume of coaches in the town and the number of grey rinses and plastic macs around, for those occasional showers. Anyway, that morning it turned out that one of the elderly holidaymakers from a coach trip had unfortunately died in the night. An occurrence that was to happen once more before that season ended.

Taking this job as a chambermaid was a smack in the eye to Mum if I'm truthful. She had never wanted me to go to grammar school in the first place and when it came to my going up into the sixth form, the arguments really started. Whilst everyone else was striving for a future at college or university to forge out a career as a teacher, engineer, or pharmacist, I was facing a losing battle. I had turned sixteen and had started my A level courses, when suddenly it seemed she could take no more and insisted that I leave and get a job.

Dad didn't win the fight for me that time. All I wanted to do was to go to college, didn't know what for and that was the problem, I didn't know what I wanted to do or be. Not like Char who had a clear vision that she wanted to be a Pharmacist. After weeks of tantrums, snots, and tears, by me of course, Mum wore me down and it was futile to argue with her anymore. Even my brother Cliff's pleas on my behalf couldn't dissuade her.

So, I left school at Christmas 1967, just three months into my sixth form year, leaving my friends behind, not knowing what the future would bring. I'd tried to sneak out on my last day, not wanting any fuss, but my very last lesson was with Miss Husband the

English teacher, who spotted me trying to make a quick exit.

'*Denise Bullen, where do you think you're going?*' she shouted in front of the whole class as they were all rushing out the door, eager to start their Christmas holidays. I had no choice but to go back and talk to her. I just wanted to get home.

'*Well, Denise, I'm sorry to see you go, what are your plans now that you're leaving school?*' she said expectantly.

'*Don't know Miss, haven't got any,*' I said sheepishly.

She looked horrified that I hadn't got this master plan for my life and that was the reason for my leaving school and education so early, but she wished me well in all my endeavours, as she put it and I walked home with very mixed emotions.

I'd loved my time at Newquay Grammar and was sad to leave. I'd been middle of the road as far as academia was concerned though and my reports repeatedly said *must apply herself* or *does not work hard enough*. On one report I was 26th out of a class of 26 and the only thing I did *exceptionally good* that year was domestic science, courtesy of Mrs Curtis, the teacher.

Those lessons were held in Crantock street school, right at the other end of town. It was a long but lovely walk to get there from Edgcumbe Avenue. Along the tramlines behind the shops with that spectacular view across the bay, that I never tired of. Plus having a laugh along the way with girls like Sue Dumpleton, Linda

Kneebone and Liz Underwood, must have been the boost I needed to do well.

Not sure Mum and Dad would agree though as we had to take home the fruits of our labour and their faces were a picture as they tackled the shepherd's pie I'd made in class.

Our teachers at Newquay Grammar all wore robes and on a windy day, the sight of them trying to maintain a level of dignity whilst their billowing gowns were whipped up around their heads, was a sight to behold. We'd have a good giggle as we went for morning break to get our free bottle of milk from the crate just inside the canteen.

I had some great teachers. Mrs Tamblyn for PE, who was always tanned in Summer and wore a fur coat and gloves as she shouted instructions from the side of the hockey pitch as we froze to death in Winter.

The sports field was next to the main building in Edgcumbe avenue, with a long jump sand pit and where I'd practise the hurdles and where I did my utmost to master lacrosse, but couldn't quite get the hang of holding the stick the right way around to actually ever catch the ball. All I caught were a lot of bruises from being in the wrong place at the wrong time. Good job Mum never bought me my own lacrosse stick. It would well have been redundant.

Sports Day one year was held up at Treninnick, on the field opposite Trevithick house, so Mum and Dad had no excuse that they couldn't come and watch me over the hedge, as we lived virtually opposite. I romped home to win the 100-yard hurdles race that year. I remember being congratulated by Geoff Prior, the head boy and his pal John Case. They were a couple of years older than us, but Char and I would often bump into them around town.

To come away with six O-levels is still a mystery to me. Miss Carter was my form teacher, but it was Miss Husband and Mr Rogers who helped me pass English literature and English language. Maths was my best subject with Mr Charrot, father of Susan, a girl in my class. He was always sucking a polo mint and very handy throwing the blackboard duster or a piece of chalk if you weren't paying attention or heaven forbid talking... or was that Sarge, Mr Sargent? Both, so inspirational.

French wasn't my best subject...at all, but I managed to pass that, having had the oral part of the exam up in a tiny attic, way up in the eves. Mr Mathias for religious education and for someone that was never baptised and years later told by a Catholic priest on the eve of her marriage that she was a heathen, wonder how I'd ever passed that. Then there was Mr Lavelle I think for History, or was that Mrs Berry, another puzzle, as I can't tell my King Edwards from my King Georges!

Then there were those subjects I didn't do so well in but enjoyed the lessons with some great character teachers. Like Mr Burley for Biology who went on to write twenty-two novels featuring Inspector Wycliffe, which were the basis of the successful television series in the 1990's.

Mr Sleep, for chemistry who had all the girls swooning as he was so good looking and who played the guitar. I saw him play once up Mitchel folk club. Not my kind of music but didn't mind as I was in the front row, so the music was an incidental really as I was quite content just staring at him all evening. His claim to fame was that he had gone to college with Ralph McTell and played alongside him occasionally.

Then there were the larger than life Reg Roberts and Bruce Connock with his mis-shapen and battered nose, courtesy of playing rugby for Newquay Hornets. They both taught Geography.

But with school well and truly behind me, I'd had to sign on at the horrid, dismal dole office in January 1968. The Labour Exchange as it was called was halfway up Fore street, opposite the infamous Sailors Arms. What a harrowing experience that was. I was still painfully shy in certain situations and finding myself amid a sea of men, when I went to sign on, made me even more nervous. I'd try and shrink into the background hoping no-one would notice me, but with little privacy when talking to the assistant at the counter, I was constantly being told to speak up. Everyone could hear what you were saying.

It was a mixture of locals as well as seasonal workers who had decided to stay in Newquay for the Winter, desperate to get their dole money so they didn't have to go back home up country. It was noisy, busy, and intimidating. I hated it. Mum wanted me to become a hairdresser or work in an office and I was ready to take any job they offered me just to avoid having to go through that trauma every week. But there were limits.

If you were sent for a job interview, you couldn't refuse, otherwise you'd lose your dole money, not like it is today, where people seem to be able to refuse the interview let alone the job. So due to my education and six O-levels to my credit, I was sent for an interview in the Post Office in Truro, to work on the counter.

Mum came with me, but when they explained what the job was and showed me the massive daily sheet that had to be completed containing every single transaction, I was petrified. It was the consequences of making a mistake and having to make up any shortfall that I didn't at all relish. It sounded too much like the constraints of school for my liking, so although I was offered the job and even though Mum wanted me to take it, I made an excuse that I didn't think I could handle it and declined. I wasn't ready for quite such a challenge.

I took an office job in John Julian's furniture showroom opposite the Victoria Hotel, a few weeks later, so I didn't have to suffer the Labour exchange for a moment longer than I had to. But I knew I wouldn't be there long. At least it kept Mum off my back for a time, while I made another plan. It was a big store over two floors, and I had my own little office at the back to work in as a ledger clerk. They were also an Estate Agents and removals firm. The staff were friendly enough and the job was relatively easy when I got the hang of it, I was responsible for entering purchases and sending bills out to customers.

I'm sure though that some customers must have got away without paying for their goods, because if I didn't know what to do with an invoice, or a docket, for any reason, I'd shove it down the back of the desk out of sight, too embarrassed to ask anyone for help. When there was nothing to do, I was bored, so instead of just clock watching I'd have a wander around the store. The stylish three-piece suites, the unmistakeable smell of new carpet and the real wood furniture, were all lost on me, even though they had been pointed out as being top quality merchandise.

I pretended to be interested and conscientious, but I was really planning for a quick departure once the hotels started advertising for staff. Mum had made me leave school against my will, so I was damned sure I was going to have some fun and to me that meant working in a hotel.

I'd seen for years, how hotel workers seemed to have it all. Getting paid for working just a few hours and then going the beach. What wasn't to like?

John Julian's closed for lunch for an hour, so I'd go for a wander through town if the weather allowed just so I didn't have to endure the pain of sitting in the staff room, head bowed, eating the cheese and Branston pickle sandwich Mum had made me. Not wanting to speak or knowing what to say if anyone spoke to me.

Out the front of the store, I'd turn right, cross over the road, past the Victoria hotel and head towards the Great Western Beach, my favourite haunt. Nine times out of ten, there would be a wet suited surfer out braving the elements, so I'd watch from the seats halfway down, getting windswept by the ferocious Atlantic winds usually. On one such trip, I noticed a nice-looking dark-haired lad painting the railings outside the Beachcroft Hotel.

I could tell he was an out-of-towner; they just had a demeanour, dress and attitude that smacked of hotel worker. He didn't even glance in my direction the first day, but as the week went on, we made eye contact, then nodded, then smiled. He had a lovely cheeky smile. I like to think he took longer than he should have painting those railings, but after a week the railings were finished, and he was gone. We never did get around to speaking as my flirting skills were still zero, so yet another brief encounter was over before it had even begun. I did see him around the town a few times after that and although we acknowledged each other, it never went any further. But that was the nature of things. You'd see seasonal hotel workers around, not really knowing them, but indirectly they became part of your world.

I was only at John Julian's for three months when I got a job interview at the St. Brannock's Hotel on Narrowcliff as a chambermaid. It was nine pound a week, but when I found out it was split shifts and I'd have to go back in the evenings, that put me off, so was over the moon when I got the job in the Minerva Hotel, in the Crescent overlooking Towan beach, which was mornings only, so only seven pound per week.

I started that first day with some trepidation though at meeting new people yet again, but I was more than ready for the adventure ahead. I worked six days a week from seven until twelve each morning, but on a Saturday, changeover day I didn't finish until gone two. It would be a right frenzy that day especially when the coach parties were in because it would be every room checking out on the same day.

In high season, although it was still Saturday departures, it may have been only half of your rooms one week and the other half the next week, so not quite as frantic, but still busy enough.

Beds would be stripped first, sheets, some occasionally with unmentionable stains that would put you off your breakfast. In high season, towels with lipstick and suntan lotion all over and pillowcases, streaked with mascara, all dumped outside in the corridor for Mrs Boxer to collect. Then it would be a thorough clean of the rooms, toilets, bathrooms and lastly hoovering throughout.

But before you did any of that, the very *first* thing you did in a room, was to look to see if they'd left you a tip. If they had, however small, it made your day.

You didn't get much from the coach parties, because it was a bargain holiday to begin with and you got the impression that most of them didn't have the cash to throw around, but to get a small tip from those elderly guests was the most rewarding.

They were the least messy, everything was in its place on the dressing table, clothes all hung up and they usually made their own beds, which was a huge help. So thankful were they for getting waited on, having their room cleaned, meals provided and not having to wash a dish. Despite the false teeth and the smell of age sometimes encountered in their rooms, they were my favourite guests. Always had a smile for you.

But in the height of summer, when the coach parties were long gone, I found that the messier and dirtier the occupants of my rooms were, the less likely it was they'd leave you anything at all. They obviously considered it was my job to clean up after them and that's what I was getting paid for.

My heart would sink if there was no tip. I'd search the dressing table and bedside table, just to make sure and feel deflated if they were empty.

Zilch, no thank you note, no appreciation for picking up after them.

Did they not realise that hotel staff got paid a pittance, such painfully low wages and relied on tips to boost their income?

Miserable so and so's!

Chatty chambermaids

The first thing I did when I started work at the Minerva, was to go back to His Casuals and this time I kept the pair of Levi jeans I'd been longing for. But they weren't without their challenges. The denim was as stiff as a board. So incredibly rigid, that the best way to soften them up and to shrink them to fit, was to lie in a bath of cold water. With them on.

When they dried, you then had to lay on the floor, and pull the zip up with the prong of a fork before you had any chance of doing up the top button. They gradually started to soften after a few cold baths, but they didn't half fit in all the right places, pulling in your tummy and backside like a corset on steroids. I've only ever worn Levi's. Still wear them today, but the denim isn't the same. Not sure if that's a good or a bad thing.

Our house at the top of Treninnick Hill had its advantages, it was quiet, peaceful, out of the way of all the hustle and bustle of the town and virtually hidden amongst a sea of trees. I loved the early mornings, when the birds twittered in the branches, the doves we'd inherited from Mrs Hook, the previous owner cooed in their outdoor cage, next to Dad's shed. The air was still, the sun was rising as the day sleepily came to life and everything in the world seemed calm and tranquil, before all hell broke loose, and the day descended into mayhem and chaos as the hordes of holidaymakers thronged the streets and beaches. The main disadvantage of living at the top of this mountainous hill was that public transport was a no go, so walking everywhere became my way of life, but I didn't mind that at all. I was used to it.

By this time, I'd been relegated to sleeping in an old caravan, Dad had bought and parked in the car park next to the old barn. When my sister Frances got married and left, the twin-bedded room we'd shared downstairs each summer, was thought too valuable for me to have to myself, so yet again, I was moved out and holidaymakers moved in.

The caravan had no electric or water, so it was just for sleeping and I had to make do with a couple of large torches to make sure I didn't bang my head or trip over something whilst moving around inside or getting ready for bed.

Each morning I'd sneak over to the house in my pyjamas, get a quick wash, grab a biscuit and a mug of tea, run back to the caravan to get dressed and be ready to start my walk into town by 6.30 a.m., down the steep Treninnick Hill, dotted with clusters of sweet smelling honeysuckle in the height of Summer.

With no pavements, woe betide if there were cars going up *and* down, passing each other along the narrow lane at the same time.

The only course of action to avoid getting mown down was to shove myself up against the brambly hedge, with the vehicles whipping past my bare legs. Well whipping is a slight exaggeration as the one in five gradient didn't allow cars to whip anywhere when coming up the hill as most engines could be heard frantically struggling to climb the mountain looming in front of them.

First gear was the only gear of choice, so Dad said. Walking down it, I'd fight against breaking into a trot, it was so steep and after passing Treforda road on the left and going under the dark canopy of trees that enveloped the bottom of the hill, I'd emerge into the bright early morning sunshine again, pausing for a minute at Trenance Gardens, to catch my breath before embarking on the next challenge. The scaling of Trenance Hill opposite.

In the valley between these two hills, the vibrant colours of the extensive and impeccably neat flower beds of Trenance gardens, to the right, were beautifully laid out as they stretched towards the Viaduct, the imposing and ancient rail structure which stood high above the road.

To the left was Trenance Lake where we'd loved messing about on the paddle boats as kids.

'Morning Mr Magpie,' I'd say, seeing a black bird in the distance, hoping that I'd spot another one *for joy* as the saying goes. The Swans and ducks would be nestled sleepily in amongst the reeds as the lake rippled slightly around them in the light breeze. The climb up Trenance Hill would be the most challenging part of my walk as it really was a mountain to climb and you just had to grit your teeth and go for it.

There was an overwhelming urge to stop for a breather halfway up just as the *mountain* turned the bend. But the fear was that a loss of footing at this stage would have sent me hurtling back down the hill like one of those balls of tumbleweed you see rolling through an empty cowboy town, in the movies. No, you just had to keep going, leaning into the hill was the only way forward, but at least this was a proper road with houses either side and pavements, so that was a bonus.

Once at the top I'd stop to catch my breath again and suck in the salty breeze drifting up from the sea. I'd cut through back alleys across the Mayfield estate, down the side of the Sutherland Hotel onto Mount Wise, down Marcus Hill, passing Polkinghorns garage, towards the bus station. Passing Land, Sea and Air travel agents and Doctor Hickey's surgery on the left-hand corner. He wasn't our Doctor, ours was Doctor Collins, a lovely lady in Trebarwith Crescent.

You didn't have to make an appointment, just arrive, sit in the surgery, and wait your turn which went in order of who got there first. You'd be disappointed if there were already quite a few people in the surgery before you as you were seen in strict order. None of this phoning the surgery for an appointment malarkey.

The Minerva Hotel was in a fantastic position overlooking the Killacourt, a lush green space in the centre of town. So named it is thought from the words Celtic Killas, meaning grove and Quoit meaning burial ground. With its colourful flower beds, crazy golf and spectacular views, perfect for sitting on a bench, lazily staring out to sea, or across to the Atlantic Hotel sitting

majestic on top of the headland. With the Huers's hut, the old fisherman's lookout just below that to one side of the vista and the famous Jagos's Island house with its connecting bridge to the mainland on the other.

That breath-taking view always made me feel lucky to be living in Newquay, so I'd pause, just for a minute to watch the sands being gently washed by the Atlantic Ocean as the waves ebbed and flowed.

My Auntie Lena, Mum's sister, who visited us many times on holiday from London, spent hours here, sitting in her deckchair, going a deep mahogany in the glorious sunshine whilst my Uncle Frank, who wasn't one for just sitting, would have a wander. Bringing back Mathew's Pasties for their lunch or a creamy Cornish cornet, courtesy of Macari's ice-cream parlour. Her and my Uncle Frank were always bickering, but they'd been married for years and that was part of their make-up. Proper Cockneys, their banter would make me laugh and I loved their visits.

There were never many people around on my morning walk into work, except girls like me rushing along in their black tops and skirts, carrying a little white apron. This was the uniform of both waitresses and chambermaids, so you soon got to know who the workers were. I usually took jeans and flip flops to change into as I didn't want to be walking back home in my 'uniform' come lunchtime and that was what I was wearing when I bumped into Sue, a girl I knew from the Blue Lagoon.

'You've even got brown feet,' she said, looking me up and down, admiring my tan. I'd been walking past Newquay Watch and Clock centre at the start of Bank street when I'd bumped into her. I could hear the envy in her voice. She wasn't a close friend, but I'd hang out with her and her pals on a Saturday night, if Char couldn't make it, so I didn't look like Billy no mates.

'How do you get so brown?'

She was still at school and here I was, having finished my shift, going home to sunbathe in the garden and get even browner.

Life wasn't so bad after all.

I'd been flummoxed on my first day at the Minerva, when Mrs B told me my *station* was just at the top of the stairs. I didn't have a clue what she was talking about. Mary had to explain to me what it meant.

Apparently, the term *station* originates from the 'wait station', which is the nerve centre of a busy dining room. Each waiter would have their own *station*, determined by the set of tables they would serve, with a dresser or cabinet or table close by, where they'd keep essentials such as spare cutlery and plates, serving dishes, napkins, to save them always having to run back to the kitchen. They would each be responsible for checking their own *station* was fully stocked before every meal, so that service could run smoother and quicker.

Woe betide anyone interfering with another person's station!

Chambermaids borrowed the term and used it to determine their set of rooms and their area of responsibility.

Every morning when I arrived at the hotel, the cups and saucers, jug of milk and bowl of sugar cubes were waiting for me, laid out on a huge table at my *station*, on the first floor ready for the guest's morning tea.

Buxom Mrs Boxer would appear, looking immaculate as always in tweed skirt, cardigan buttoned up to the neck, pearls, sensible shoes, and hair in a neat bun, carrying a huge pot of freshly brewed tea.

I'd pour each cup, add milk, and put two sugar cubes and spoon in each saucer. Then I'd carefully carry them to each door, knock and walk in shouting *'morning tea'*. Bearing in mind that many of the guests were hard of hearing, they didn't hear me knock, so some would get a fright when I suddenly appeared. Many a time I had to slide a glass full of false teeth aside to make room for the cup on the bedside table or gently nudge someone awake. The smell of Wintergreen or Vick would be overpowering. I was so nervous when I first started that the tea would slosh into the saucer, dissolving the sugar cubes, before I even got to their doors.

The Minerva was typical of an older established seaside hotel, busy patterned carpets, dark wood furniture and a sink in every bedroom with bathrooms and toilets down the hall. Corridors going every which way, round hidden corners, twists and turns up and down stairs, you could easily get lost. We three had our own set of rooms, ten or so each, which we were responsible for cleaning each day.

I only had one room that overlooked the sea. it was a small single and I thought how lucky that person was to have such a fabulous view over the Killacourt. I was very conscientious at first, making sure I made all the beds correctly, with a housewife's corner as Mum had taught me, emptying bins, cleaning sinks, and hoovering every room *every* day. A proper Miss Goody Two Shoes, but that soon changed when Mary and Kathy got the measure of me. They were little devils.

We three became great friends. I would try to mimic their soft Irish accent, which I never quite mastered, which made them laugh. In return they taught me loads and became my co-conspirators as well as my mentors. They had been at the Minerva for a few years, so knew all the tricks and shortcuts which made our days very enjoyable.

After my initial over exuberance at doing everything correctly, they soon showed me the minimum amount of work needed to be done each day. So that we could use our *'spare time'* to sit on the stairs, drink shed loads of tea, which we could make in the little kitchenette on the first floor, where we washed all the cups, have a natter and put the world to rights and give Kathy the chance to light up a Rothmans.

We'd position ourselves carefully, so that we could quickly scatter if we heard Mrs Boxer coming, frantically waving away any lingering cigarette smoke and start hoovering to look busy. Mostly though she left us alone to get on with it.

The only days we were really busy was when one of us had our day off and the other two had to clean their set of rooms as well as our own or on a Saturday, the only changeover day back then. None of this three- or four-day lark, it was seven or fourteen days or nothing, when one set of holidaymakers would leave, and another would arrive. That was frantic. The downside was that we wouldn't get finished until after two that day.

Another perk was trying all the lotions and potions the guests brought with them. Not so much the elderly guests, but in high season, guests would be of all ages, so having a quick spray of a perfume or trying a face cream was obligatory for chambermaids. I can remember someone having Selsun dandruff shampoo and having suffered the same complaint did consider washing my hair to try it out but didn't think I'd get away with that one. Mary on the other hand was braver than me and one day did just that, used a guest's shampoo, leaving her hair to dry whilst finishing her shift.

I loved my time at the Minerva and loved my chats with Mary and Kathy, so was delighted that at the end of that summer we all got chambermaid jobs at the prestigious Bristol Hotel, for the Winter, one of only a handful that stayed open all year. Our adventures were about to continue.

Perhaps Mum was right though after all, about her career aspirations for me, to become a hairdresser or work in an office. Because all my life I have been passionate about having nice hair and years later in my career did in fact join the Post Office!

Christmas cry baby

'*Do you want Dad to come and get you, he can be there in about fifteen minutes?*' Mum said.

'*No, I'll have to be back in a couple of hours, it's not worth it,*' I said trying my hardest not to cry.

It was Christmas Day, 1968 and I'd just walked home to Treninnick House after an exhausting morning shift as a chambermaid in the Bristol Hotel. Mum and Dad had gone to my sister Frances and Alan's house for Christmas lunch down Kestle Mill. Roast turkey and all the trimmings and I'd gone home to an empty house and a plate of ham salad left in the fridge. It was half past three in the afternoon. I'd even missed the Queen's speech. Not that I was an avid watcher any other Christmas, but it was another milestone in the day that had passed me by.

I cried as soon as I put the phone down. I knew no-one would be home, just hadn't realised how desolate that would make me feel. The first Christmas Day I had ever had to work and with no lights on or warmth of the fire to welcome me home, the spookiness of the old house together with daylight fading fast, it made for a very dismal afternoon.

I was almost glad to get back to work that evening, to turn the beds down. The turndown service was a sign, to me, that the Bristol was a high-class hotel intent on providing the best possible customer experience.

As soon as all the residents had all gone down for evening dinner, I would have a list of rooms that had requested this service, plus if anyone had requested extra towels or pillows or such like. I'd do a quick tidy around of each room, empty bins, give the sink a quick going over if necessary, and then finally make the bed if it had been used during the day and then turn it down. This consisted of turning down the sheet, blanket and bedspread, altogether, forming a neat right-angled triangle by the pillow, to allow for ease of access. The same on the other side for a double bed. It wasn't a particularly arduous task, just a pain, always having to work split shifts. You felt the days were never your own, knowing you always had to go back to work in the evenings. If I hadn't had to go back to work that day, I could have had an enjoyable Christmas dinner with the family instead.

At least Mum and Dad would be back by the time I finally got home. I was proper feeling sorry for myself and this Christmas had been a rude awakening to what adult working life was all about. My time at the Minerva had just been the starter. This was now most definitely the main course. I cried a few more times that afternoon, before trudging back to work.

The Bristol was *the* hotel in Newquay, or at least one of them and one of the few open all year around so to get a job for the Winter was a major achievement. The building, with its red brickwork and contrasting cream window frames, stands in a superior position on

Narrowcliff having spectacular views across Newquay Bay, far out into the Atlantic.

Keeping watch over Tolcarne Beach and taking the brunt of all that the weather throws at her, whether basking in glorious sunshine or battered by dashing rain and howling winds as it whistles around her ramparts.

During my teenage years, Mum and I had come to blows a few times, not literally, but arguments serious enough to make a huge dent in our previously cordial relationship. Making me leave school though, was by far the biggest.

While all my friends were starting their A levels, I was signing on at the Labour exchange. While they were all striving to further their education at college or university, I was job hunting and while they were all embracing academia, I was scrubbing toilet seats.

Having said that though, I still considered myself lucky to have gotten this chambermaid's job, otherwise it would have been the gruesome task of signing on at the dole office again in Fore Street every Thursday morning. With tourism the main industry in Cornwall at the time, Newquay, like many other seaside resorts, hibernated each Winter from October through to Easter each year.

Hotels and Guest houses closed, most seasonal staff went back to their homes up country, bedrooms were left to gather dust and linens were moth balled and stashed away until the following summer season, when it started all over again.

I'd left the Minerva and had a couple of weeks off, going up to London with Mum and Dad as usual, before I started, late October. Mary and Cathy were already there, so at least I was with familiar faces, but really didn't know what to expect. I was feeling anxious about that first day as I went through the front door into reception.

At the end of the day, a chambermaid is a chambermaid, no matter where you work, right?

After all, changing beds and cleaning up after people can't be that different depending on where you work, can it?

Well at the Bristol, there was an air of expectation, of old-fashioned grandeur, a feeling that you were walking into somewhere special, which immediately set it apart from other hotels.

The Bristol had been in the Young family since about 1927 and Mr Stuart Young was running it, with other members of the family including his great aunt Mrs Francis. I would have to clean her bedroom occasionally and was shocked to find her squashed into the smallest of rooms.

I'd expected her to have one of the best sea-facing rooms in the hotel. Even though she was nice to me, I was a little in awe of her, being one of the bosses. When I saw that even she had to make a sacrifice for the good of paying guests, I realised that perhaps we weren't so different after all, as I'd had to do the same for years.

I was put on general cleaning duties at first, as after a summer packed to the rafters, the rooms needed a good going over before the Winter season took hold with its conferences, functions, banquets, and Christmas celebrations.

'*What are ya doing, you've been ages, so you have,*' said my Irish mate Cathy, poking her head around the bathroom door, scaring me half to death, making me drop the toilet brush.

'*Is this your first room, is it?*' she added.

I was on my own on the top floor, wanting to make it spotless, so I'd been thorough. I was glad to see a friendly face, the hotel was that big and sprawling, I'd only seen the head housekeeper up to that point, who had sent me up there. I hadn't seen another soul for a few hours, so wondered if I'd wandered into the Marie Celeste, as I had expected it to be bustling. Yes, I thought, I can handle this. Little did I know, this was the calm before the storm.

'*She's after looking for ya,*' she added. Then hearing footsteps, she poked her head back out the door.

'*Here's herself now, so it is,*' and with that she was gone.

'*You'll have to speed up Denise. Far too slow,*' said the Head Housekeeper, inspecting the room, realising that was the only one I'd completed. But after a week or two, I soon got into the swing of things and got my own station on the first floor. With some huge sprawling rooms to clean as well as the long wide corridors, it felt like you were having to clean a whole street, day after day, but they weren't all occupied. It was a gradual slow burn up until Christmas.

Not many of the rooms were en-suite in those days, with bathrooms along each corridor. Every room inspected by the housekeeper before new guests arrived and before you could go home. I dreaded her coming around with that clipboard of hers and not getting a tick against my rooms.

I soon realised that those nice long homely chats, Mary, Cathy, and I had enjoyed on the stairs in the Minerva, were things of the past, and this was all about work, work, work. The only time we really got together was at breakfast times.

One of the worst parts of the job was bringing the guests breakfast in bed, which luckily wasn't that often. My heart would sink when I arrived at seven in the morning, having just walked the one and a half miles from home in the pitch black. Under the viaduct, past the site where the town's zoo, was due to open in the May of 1969, the following year.

I was positive they'd got a few animals in there ahead of opening, as where else would the roars and grunts be coming from? I'd rush past the tennis courts and bowling green and on up Ulalia road to the Bristol. Running the last two hundred yards, because I'd heard footsteps behind me in the dark, only to find the dreaded breakfast in bed requests for me in the staff room.

Then the Christmas weekend arrived. There was a buzz about the place that was exciting. At first. The Hill family occupied the largest and plushest corner room on my floor, with sumptuous red and gold soft furnishings.

The four days of Christmas celebrations at the Bristol Hotel I gathered weren't cheap, but you get what you pay for as they say. Guests were pampered rotten in every respect, with the focus being on food, food, and more food with entertainment thrown in. If the full English breakfast, morning coffee and three course lunch wasn't enough to satisfy their appetites, there was afternoon tea and then canapés before the seven-course evening dinner! The men all dressed in evening suits and the women in long frocks, 'rattling their jewellery', a saying made famous by John Lennon at the London Palladium in 1963. Dancing the night away to the orchestra brought in for the festivities.

Not my kind of thing. In the early 60s I'd swooned over the Beatles, been mesmerised by the gyrating hips of Mick Jagger, but had moved on from those schoolgirl crushes and was now swaying to the 'Sweet Soul Music' of Tamla Motown. 'Getting on down' at the Blue Lagoon. Dancing was my stress buster.

The Hills had interconnecting bedrooms, one for the parents and the other for their two small sons, with a bathroom next door. The family had arrived the day before Christmas eve and I knew they were going to be trouble from that first evening, when I'd gone to turn down the beds. It should only have been a quick in and out, but I had to virtually remake all the beds, clean the sink, empty the bins and pick up clothes strewn across chairs, chaise longue and overflowing open drawers.

Christmas morning was the worst though, they had ordered breakfast in bed, my nemesis on any normal day, let alone that day. Whilst they were all having a relaxing lie-in, I was having to haul a mega heavy tray up the slippery wrought iron back stairs, just so they didn't have to endure the bother of getting dressed and going downstairs to the dining room.

Usually, if it was an early breakfast request, the kitchens were relatively quiet at that time in the morning but it was still daunting for someone who had never stepped inside a large professional working hotel kitchen before, with steam coming at you from every direction. Fierce bright lights with grumpy chefs and waiters getting ready for the breakfast onslaught.

'Two full English,' I said in the general direction of the chef, expecting a carving knife to come hurtling past my earlobe any second. Chefs were renowned for being cantankerous and bad-tempered, but the breakfast chefs seemed to be the worst and this one was no exception. Wishing him *'Good morning,'* was a no-no and making eye contact was a sure sign the eggs would be broken, the bacon burnt and the fried bread swimming in grease.

'You'll have to shout louder than that,' said the good-looking dark-haired waiter from Liverpool who was busy filling the cruets for the dining tables. I hadn't noticed him when I'd walked in. Some of the waiters on early shift would help, to make sure you had everything you needed, and he was particularly helpful. I could feel myself going red.

'Two full English,' I shouted again and chef looked up this time, but he still didn't move until he'd taken another sly swig from the Watney's Party seven, left over from the night before, which he'd stashed behind the toaster. I laid up the tray with a tray lining

and linen serviettes, heavy silver teapot, filled from a hot water contraption that you'd scald your hands on if you didn't concentrate. The sugar bowl I'd made sure was full of sugar cubes with little silver tongs, jug of milk, cereal bowls full of cornflakes, glasses of orange juice, cutlery, cruet and a rack of piping hot toast just in time for the breakfasts to be loaded on. One on top of the other using a plate divider, with a closed one on top to keep them warm. Despite his best efforts to the contrary I eventually got two decent looking breakfasts from the chef.

The iron fire escape that I had to climb with the laden tray, was treacherous. Although partially covered by a decorative overhanging glass canopy, the wind and rain could still whip in, so when both arms were fully employed carrying the massive tray, you had no free hand to wipe away the hair blown into your eyes.

Very often you were blind for the last few steps and had to tentatively feel your way with your feet. Opening the fire door to get access to your floor was another obstacle and there was nothing for it, but to put the tray down, open the door, keep it open with your bum, while you carefully lifted the tray through before it slammed shut behind you.

Despite all that, I managed to arrive at the Hill's door at precisely 8.30a.m, with tray and its contents almost intact. I on the other hand, had windswept hair, apron all askew, a burnt thumb, from the spilled water jug and I was all hot and sweaty with red cheeks and frayed nerves.

Nothing new there then.

Careful what you wish for

What I hadn't expected to find on entering the Hill's room, were the parents in an extremely compromising position, which stopped mid-flight so to speak as I entered. They obviously hadn't heard me knock. I carried on as if I hadn't noticed, trying to spot a vacant surface on which to place the now unbearably heavy tray and had to brush away bags, boxes and tinsel from the coffee table with my elbow and the side of the tray, before banging it down with relief.

The boys had obviously already been up once, then gone back to bed, as Christmas presents and wrapping paper were strewn all over the place. It was difficult not to step on Action man, demolish the Meccano set before they'd had a chance to build anything or scoot across the room on the three-wheeler bike. Goodness knows how they packed that in their suitcase!

I usually got a tangerine, selection box and make-up bag in my Christmas stocking, if I was lucky.

What a mess, was all I could think as I tiptoed back out of the room, trying not to look in their direction. *It's going to take me all morning to clean this one room.*

This was hard work at the best of times, but the holiday festivities had been punishing. Up at six each day, quick cuppa before the mile and a half walk to start at seven. Back home way past two and then walk back again by six thirty in the evening to turn down the beds and be on call for any evening requests from the guests, such as more pillows or blankets. It was usually past nine before I'd eventually get home having scaled Treninnick Hill for the second time that day. I'd be done in and go straight to bed.

There were a few perks though.

Like gradually getting to know that good-looking waiter from Liverpool despite him always making me go red.

Like going to loads of parties and nights out with the rest of the staff, once Christmas was over.

Like having a laugh with the other chambermaids at every opportunity, despite the punishing workload.

Like the delicious, cooked breakfast, we had when we stopped for a break. We'd all traipse down to the kitchen and I didn't feel so intimidated by chef when we went on mass. I'd order fried egg, crispy bacon, and soft sweet tomatoes, all slapped on to two slices of hot buttered toast to make a doorstop of a sandwich. Tomato juice trickling down my chin as I woofed it down followed by a steaming hot mug of tea and a large dollop of gossip served up in the chambermaid's staff room.

Even better though was secretly being able to try all the guests' lotions and potions. Mrs Hill had a large bottle of Tabu which I'd never smelt before. Mum only used Lily of the Valley and I hadn't really gotten into perfume. A little spray wouldn't do any harm. So, I thought.

I was nearly asphyxiated by the spicy oriental aroma as it permeated the whole room. Panicking I'd be found out, I pushed up the sash window, anticipating a waft of fresh air to dissipate the smell. But instead, the ferocious Atlantic wind sucked out the net curtain and it flew like a proud flag at the front of the building, before I could yank it back in. Not before the hotel's front doorman, looking mortified, had spotted it and was waving frantically at me, as if I hadn't noticed.

After slamming the window shut and smoothing the curtain, I hastily polished all the wood surfaces with Beeswax hoping to dowse the unmistakeable smell which despite my best efforts was still lingering.

I'd also often have a root through the guests' wardrobe, just to have a nose. I was tempted to try things on, but usually only had the courage to hold the dresses up against me to see how I'd look... as a lady. There was a particularly lovely fox fur wrap of Mrs Hill's that caught my eye and I still had it draped around my shoulders when I heard the door handle turning. Not having time to put it back in the wardrobe, I stuffed it into the nearest drawer, slamming it shut only to see its tail protruding out the corner.

'I've just come back for my coat dear, carry on, I'll be out of your way in a jiffy.'

It was the one and only time she spoke to me.

I had no choice but to move away from the offending evidence and carry on cleaning. Luckily, she soon left, and I replaced that naughty fox back in the wardrobe.

The rest of Christmas went by in a blur and I was too busy and too tired to think much about that close encounter with Mrs Hill or anything else for that matter and just when I thought it was safe....

'You're wanted Denise... down in reception.'
'But I've only just started my rooms...'
'NOW Denise and use the front stairs.'

The front stairs! I'd been told never again to use the front stairs by the head receptionist when I came in through the front door on my first day. When shifts were over, staff had to leave by the back entrance, out of sight of the paying guests. It had been one hell of a Christmas. I was worn out and fed up, just wanting to get as far away from the place as possible.

'Be careful what you wish for,' Mum always said.

The formidable Head Housekeeper...Silly Knickers, we Chambermaids called her, behind her back of course, smirked as she virtually spat the words at me. She must have enjoyed telling us off, because she did it so often, especially me. But I didn't dream of talking back to her.

What have I done now, I thought as I dumped my armful of clean sheets back on the trolley? *After all, I couldn't be expected to always get in on time, have a spotlessly clean white apron or find every speck of dust...could I? It must be serious to have been summoned like this.*

'Come on girl, don't dawdle, we haven't got all day.'

As I followed her towards the stairs, I couldn't walk too fast, as the heel of my shoe had already come flying off once that week and gone careering down the long wide corridor, leaving me hobbling in hot pursuit. The heavy brown brogues that my Dad laughingly nicknamed clodhoppers, had big square chub heels and were the latest fashion and even though Mum said they looked too big and clumsy on the end of my long skinny legs, I wasn't about to part with them in a hurry. I'd glued it back on, but it felt as wobbly and unsteady as I did at that moment in time.

Silly Knickers wasn't content with just calling me by name, but had this annoying habit of elongating it, shouting Deneeeeese up and down the corridor, so nobody was in any doubt about when I was in trouble! I was Dennie or Den to friends. Dad being a Londoner called me 'Duck' all the time and Mum's was 'Dear' or 'Love'; only Denise when I was in trouble or up to no good and when I was seventeen, that seemed to be constant. *So, is this it? Am I about to prove my Mother right yet again?* I could hear her words already.

'I said you should have taken that job in the Post Office, but oh no, you wouldn't listen, now see what's happened.'

Her recrimination was going to be worse, than *actually* getting the sack.

Surely, I can't lose this job now!

Several heads peeped out from the bedrooms as we passed by. Fellow chambermaids emerged, some holding bundles of dirty towels, others with loo brush or duster in hand. All giving me pitying looks and thanking their lucky stars that it was me and not them getting frogmarched down the corridor. Cathy, my friend, and usual partner in crime, mouthed *What have you been after doing now?* I shrugged my shoulders. Mary, our other co-conspirator, emerging from one of her rooms, went to say something to Silly Knickers, but I shook my head to stop her. Didn't want her to get in trouble as well. She pushed her thick black glasses up her nose, as they were always slipping and tutted as we passed by.

This wasn't the Minerva and it wasn't the easy-going environment I had become so accustomed to.

Was this about to end for me?

Jolting me back to reality, Silly Knickers caught my elbow and virtually manhandled me around the bend of the wide sweeping staircase as the front of house of this elegant early 1900's four-star hotel came into full view and there was the manager shaking hands with…oh my goodness no, Mr and Mrs Hill.

They were about to leave, two little boys in tow and a porter trying to manoeuvre an overloaded luggage trolley.

I'm done for now.

I hesitated as we reached the bottom, fearful of not only getting my marching orders but also of disappearing in a puff of smoke, as punishment for having used the front stairs and even worse, then stepping on to the forbidden hallowed turf of the lavish reception.

Either way, my goose is well and truly cooked!

My brain was working overtime as the manager walked towards me.

'There you are Denise,' he said. *'Mr and Mrs Hill have been telling me all about you.'*

My legs suddenly felt very weak and I thought I was going to feint, thankful for once that Silly Knickers was still hanging on to my elbow.

He was holding a brown envelope towards me.

This is it. P45 time.

My hand was shaking as I opened it. Inside was a letter.

'Dear Denise, the enclosed is for you. This is to say thank you very much for looking after us so well. You are a credit to this hotel, which we have relayed to the manager. We know it couldn't have been easy, dealing with all our mess and we appreciate your discretion in er... certain matters'.

Out dropped a five-pound note. I was shocked, dumb struck, lost for words. I read on-

'Perhaps you could buy yourself some Tabu,'
Regards,
James and Madeleine Hill
'P.S. By the way, Mr Fox says hello!'

I was gobsmacked. Even Silly Knickers gave me a smile and a little pat on my arm, although she couldn't quite bring herself to say well done, as we walked back upstairs, but it was near enough.

Christmas hadn't been so bad after all.

Party time

'You're the girl with the ice cream,' he said smiling.

It was *my* waiter. The one who always made me go red every time he spoke to me.

'I've only just realised,' he added.

He was the one that had stopped me outside Menzies that time and asked for a lick of my ice-cream and commented on my Bermuda shorts and he was one of the lads I'd seen in the King Mark, who loved to dance.

I'd only just realised.

We chambermaids hadn't had time to hang out with each other, let alone anybody else, but once the frenzy of Christmas in the Bristol was over and the hotel got back to some normality, the staff started to party. Nights out became very lively. The first of those was in-between Christmas and New Year and someone organised an impromptu party in one of the staff houses and we all chipped in for booze and a few snacks. I had on a skirt than Mum had made me and a sweater I'd knitted myself. Music was as loud as it could be without getting told off by management after previous complaints by the neighbours.

This was the first time we'd all been able to let our hair down a little.

I thought we chambermaids had it hard over that Christmas, but the dining room staff seemed to have it even worse.

Ted Rogers was the Head waiter at the time, with Alfie, his second in command, both looking dapper, always wearing tails for evening dinner service. Therefore, they expected their waiters to be just as immaculate, which they were. Wearing black dinner suit trousers with the satin stripe down each leg, crisp white shirts, cummerbunds, bow ties and short waiter's cream jackets, they all looked the part, very professional.

But their hours were punishing, with most days, starting about 8 a.m. By the time they'd finished the breakfast shift and laid up for lunch it was 11 a.m., then back on duty for 12.30 for lunch service, finish about 3 p.m., then back for Dinner at 6.30p.m., finishing about 10p.m. Not much time to get to any of the bars in town, so the long side bar of the Bristol was the nearest watering hole and became the go to place for staff.

I'd seen *my waiter* in there once when I'd gone for a drink with Margaret and Barbara, the two chambermaids from Liverpool I'd got friendly with, but he'd hardly given me a second glance.

But the night of that party, *my waiter*, Pat from Liverpool, and I had a few drinks and a few dances, as you do, getting to know each other a little better.

Going to the Sailors for their New Year's Eve fancy dress party though, was the highlight of that week for us chambermaids. We hadn't had time to turn around over the Christmas, let alone think about fancy dress costumes to wear.

So, I had taken clothes to change into after shift, a peach coloured cotton scoop necked dress with green biased binding that Mum as usual, had made me and we all got ready in Margaret and Barbara's staff room.

They'd become great pals of mine. My best friend Charmaine had come along to meet us there and we all headed off into the town, stopping off at various places, before eventually ending up at the Sailors Arms and bumping into a very fetching Pinky Tippett and almost unrecognisable Chris Jones in their very fancy dresses and wigs.

I was embarrassed to see Chris after that very brief encounter we'd had a year or so before, but he always smiled, and although that distressing episode was engraved in my memory, I hoped that he had forgotten all about it.

At seventeen, I was still not legally old enough to drink, but now hanging out with older mates, got away with a lot more and would have a gin and lime or vodka and orange, as I thought they sounded like grown up drinks.

To be honest though, I didn't like the taste of either, so there was no chance of me ever getting drunk. Mum wasn't at all happy about my new-found friends, thinking they were leading me astray, but as I was now working, she couldn't really put her foot down.

Pat Jones, *'my waiter'* from Liverpool shared his staff room with Dave Perkins who married Jackie who later became the manager of the Dorothy Perkins shop on Bank street. Tommy Caldwell from Liverpool also stayed down that winter, working at the Bristol, Tommy was a proper 'Jack the lad' always sporting a deep tan.

My first proper date with Pat was a few weeks later. I'd gone to meet him at the staff quarters at the back of the hotel and we'd planned to have a few drinks in the Bristol's side bar. We had to pass the hotel's garages on the way and with dim, limited lighting and even less moonlight, I had trouble seeing where I was going.

Disaster suddenly struck.

I'd been so preoccupied in trying to look good while the wind was destroying my carefully coiffured hair. Plus trying to act all grown up, listening intently, doing my best to understand his Liverpool accent, I hadn't noticed the open drain beside one of the garages up ahead.

My left leg suddenly disappeared down that damned drain.

He'd taken a few steps on, before he noticed I was in trouble. Having extracted my leg, I was frantically trying to wipe off the wet sodden leaves and other unmentionables that were now attached.

I was mortified.

He was trying not to laugh. I could see.

But he tried to be helpful and got out his hanky, trying to rectify the damage, by wiping away the debris as best he could. Once in the safety of the Bristol bar, I dived into the loo, disposed of my laddered tights and washed my leg. What a start I thought. Is this going to be another relationship scuppered before its even begun.

But no, we soon became an item, *'going steady'* as my Mum put it, much to her dismay.

Although this was his first Winter in Newquay, he'd been working the Summer season as a waiter, since 1965, first in the Savoia on Lusty Glaze road, which was then the only Newquay hotel that offered full silver service in the dining room. It later changed its name to the Riviera.

He did stints in the Marina and Edgcumbe hotels that same year and the following year in 1966, World cup year, was in the Grand View Hotel up Pentire. His mates came down from Liverpool that first Summer to see him, where they'd all hang out at the Tall Trees.

The following Summer he started in the Victoria hotel on East street, another grand Newquay hotel, perched in a superb position on the cliff top, having spectacular views of the Bay. At one time it boasted as being the only hotel that had direct lift access from all its floors down to the beach far below.

Mrs Boyden owned the Victoria, who, I believe, was the sister-in-law of Stuart Young of the Bristol. Nobby Clark was the manager. Then there were the two Miss Knapp sisters, one worked in the office at the Bristol and the other at the Victoria.

Sheila, whose first husband was the manager of the Savoia and who later went on to marry Mr Whitehouse, the jeweller of Central Square, was another member of the office staff.

Peter the chef went on to own the Crigga Bay hotel and Tommy Harris was the second chef. Terry Lewis was the head waiter and with his wife Margaret, later owned a hotel on Mount Wise.

Then there was Tony and Josie Cobley, who later went on to own several hotels around the town, including the Atlantic Hotel.

They all worked with Pat in the dining room.

He'd take me to the Hoi Gan Chinese restaurant opposite 'The Vic' which he called the Victoria hotel, where I first tasted Lychee. Or we'd have a drink in the Croft Bar in the Beachcroft hotel. Lovely hotel, sadly no longer there, but where the Aldi now stands.

Or we'd pop up the steps to the Prince Albert bar at the side of the Vic, where we'd usually spot Tommy Guinness, a kitchen porter, who was usually propping up the bar. Don't think that was his real name, as like many of the characters around the town, that's what he was known as. Kitchen porter being the fancy name for the hotel pot washer.

Sunday nights at the Doublestiles Pub up St. Columb Minor was a regular night out and it used to get packed. Bar on the top level, then down a few stairs to the dance floor, where the Coconut Grove would be playing, more often than not.

'Is he still going out with her?' I heard a girl say to her mate, in there one night as Pat and I walked past. I must admit, we must have made an unlikely match.

There was Pat always smartly dressed in bespoke three-piece suits. There was me in my bright ruby red Wrangler jacket that I'd bought from the little boutique on the corner of Beachfield avenue. Flair I think the shop was called.

Pat, outgoing, gregarious, streetwise, had seen the world with the merchant navy, huge family, loads of friends and could talk to anyone.

Me, introvert, shy, naïve, a member of the make do and mend brigade, small group of close friends, limited trips abroad and would get tongue-tied and embarrassed at regular intervals.

But somehow the love affair with *'my Liverpool waiter'* flourished.

Treninnick Tavern

'Quick,' said Dad running in from the restaurant, *'Towels, I need towels, there's water pouring under the front door'*...

I don't know if it was their plan all along to open a Pub, but Dad loved a challenge and probably egged on by Mum, that's exactly what they did. But it was a slow process achieving this latest dream and it had to be approached in stages with a few big hurdles to overcome along the way. After running Treninnick as a guest house for a couple of years, the first stage was for Dad with the help of my brother Cliff to build a large two-story extension on the left-hand side of the house.

To get planning permission it had to be in keeping with the rest of the building, so it had whitewashed walls to the exterior, pitched roof, windows with shutters and a Cornish stone porch. There were three bedrooms and a bathroom upstairs, so even more rooms to let out to holidaymakers. Downstairs was one big room with beams to match the main house and bench seating in the booths that lined the two Cornish stone clad walls, a small bar and the Ladies and Gents toilets were at the back.

Dad had built the extension specifically for the purpose of opening a restaurant as this was the only route at the time to him getting a full license to open a Pub. Therefore, a Supper license was applied for, which meant they could serve alcohol, but only with a meal. He'd knocked through the three-foot-thick wall of the main house to connect the back of the bar in the new restaurant extension to the back of the bar he'd built in the lounge of the main house. But it was one hell of a job. It took him forever.

The lounge in the main house, then became the waiting area where customers could have a pre-meal drink before then going through to the restaurant. He'd also laid beer pipes going from the bar to the garage which then became the beer cellar with its draught beer kegs, bottled ales, and gas bottles. They did okay in the restaurant, some big parties came to eat. Mum was a great cook, not a chef, so the menu was good food, nothing fancy, but one thing that sticks with me is how she made her chips.

She made them from a potato mix that then went through a machine and chip shapes came out the other end on to a tray which she then cooked in the oven. I always thought this was a bit odd not using actual potatoes, but customers came back, so they must have liked them.

Both the main house and the restaurant extension were in a dip and there were two steps down as you walked into both from the front doors. It had been torrential rain that evening when Dad screamed for the towels. The torrent of water from the day's relentless downpours had cascaded down the steps from the carpark, down the sloping concrete path, under the door and straight down the steps into the restaurant. So, whilst customers were tucking into their steak and chips that night, poor Dad was trying to stem the deluge of water flooding in.

Being Dad, he soon solved that problem, but they had to let customers in through the main house door for a few days until the carpet dried out.

After running the restaurant for a year or so, he then applied for the full alcohol license and yet another hurdle had to be overcome. He was advised to get as much support for opening a Pub as possible, in case there was opposition in the area, which at the time was anticipated from the King's Head up at Lane, together with the Mellanvrane hotel, down the bottom of Mellanvrane lane. We also found out there was the Lanherne in Ulalia road going for a full license at the same time, so we had to get all our ducks in a row, to give us the best possible chance.

Plus, there was Trevithick House and Treninnick farm close by that could have been potentially worried about additional traffic noise passing their properties and of course Mr. Gerber, my Grammar school headmaster, who lived just around the corner. Didn't know what he was going to think.

To that end, the whole family were dispatched with clip boards with a bit of a spiel about the benefits of having a Pub in the area, to gauge the re-action. But also, to get as many signatures on the petition as possible. There I was, yet again, having to knock on doors and got that same nervy, anxious feeling when I had to speak face to face with strangers. There was nowhere near the number of houses in Treninnick as there are now, but still a fair few to get around.

Dad got the full license and named the Pub, Treninnick Tavern. It opened in 1969.

Opening hours were 12-2 and 6-10.30. No all-day opening back then. As the Pub lay in a dip and couldn't be seen from the main road, it took word of mouth to get things going but trade gradually started to pick up, particularly from locals. Mum did bar-food, which was Cheese or Ham ploughman's or Pasties plus Chicken or Scampi in the basket of an evening.

It was a Free house, so not tied to any brewery, so they could sell what ales and brands they liked. There was draught Worthington E and Watney's Red Barrel, VAT 69 whisky, Booths Gin, Harp lager and of course Babycham.

Jim Dale the Bass rep worked behind the bar some lunchtimes as did his wife.

The bell that Dad rung for last orders was the large cowbell he'd brought back from Switzerland. He must have known it would come in handy sometime.

The till was just a drawer under the counter, reminiscent of the Grocer's shop and mental arithmetic, the order of the day, when it came to adding up somebody's bill. There were no prices on anything, you just got to know what everything cost, and it became second nature.

Lunchtimes were always slow, if nice weather, as holidaymakers would be on the beach, but Treninnick

Tavern steadily became a great local community Pub, particularly in the evenings and weekends.

Airmen from St. Mawgan who were housed up Treloggan, became regulars, like Bill and Charmaine. The Stanton family that bought our bungalow opposite, in Middleton crescent were frequent customers as were Lou and Judith who lived a few doors up from them.

Dad wasn't a natural front man. He was more comfortable behind the scenes.

His somewhat dour, hangdog expression gave off a false impression sometimes until customers got to know him and soon warmed to his humour and friendliness.

But he rose to the challenge and like all Pubs, the locals loved to see and have a chat with the landlord. Obligatory if you want to do well. He wasn't even much of a drinker. He'd only take 20p or so when customers said, *'Take your own'* and his one half a beer would sit there all night, hardly touched. He'd always look smart though, sporting a white shirt and tie.

Locals such as Adrian Caldwell, who went to Newquay Grammar with me, his brother Paul, their Mum Pat, and stepdad Joe, who lived in a cottage behind the Tavern. Ron Doyle the photographer and his wife who were friends with Alan and Frances. Then there was Scots Mat who delivered gas bottles around the town, always a jolly chap. He used to come in with his landlady Gladys. He became part of the woodwork like so many others and their own pint pots had their own hooks above the bar.

You'd get to know what they drank and whose pot was whose, so if you saw them coming through the front door, their pint was almost pulled by the time they reached the bar. There was Ron and Win Kennett, a double diamond salesman, who, lived in Cleveland road, where Cliff had his house.

There was Geoff and Barbara Cook and John Cann, who all became great friends with my brother Cliff and his wife Chris. Brian and Ann Taylor who went to live on Gozo and many, many more.

I was eighteen by this time, so could legally serve, when I wasn't working in the Central Hotel, where I'd started that April, after leaving the Bristol. Still shy, I'd be hard pressed at first to make eye contact as it felt like I was again, far too up close and personal serving in the small bar. There was no room for more than two of us at any one time without tripping over each other.

I gradually got used to it and more often than not a local or two would be standing at the end, so they'd become friends as well as customers, with whom you could have a laugh and a chat. Regulars up in the restaurant bar on a Saturday night included Bert and Doug, who I loved serving as Bert had such an infectious laugh, it made working much more enjoyable.

Dad eventually got a sign up the top on the corner of the main road with an arrow pointing down to the Pub, so that holidaymakers would spot it and he had postcards printed and key rings made to giveaway as a reminder of their visit and hopefully tell others.

The chairs by the roaring fire in the main lounge in Winter would be sought after, but it was the dart board down the other end that attracted a lot of customers, like Chris Cross who was a great darts player.

Both men's and ladies' darts teams were formed as well as football teams and there would be a table or two of euchre getting played most nights in the restaurant bar. Pork Scratchings were the snack of the moment.

The highlight of the year had to be the fancy dress party on New Year's Eve. Philip Schofield's brother would do the music for the evening and almost everybody joined in, with some amazing outfits with prizes for the best. It was packed out and a great atmosphere.

All the family regularly helped in the Pub when we could. My sister Frances and Alan would move in and run the place when Mum and Dad went away on holiday. Mum liked cruising by this time, particularly with the

Fred Olson line. Dad wasn't so keen I don't think, but he indulged Mum as she could dress up and dance and wear the couple of wigs, she liked to take with her.

Mum's afternoon naps continued, wherever we lived, and it was just as well that the Pub closed in the afternoons, so that she could continue with that practice. But when her bouts of Brucellosis kicked in, once or twice a year, she was rendered helpless and confined to her bed for days at a time, so it was all hands to the pump, when that happened.

She'd get a terrible fever, awful joint pain, and debilitating fatigue. She always assumed, she'd caught the disease through drinking unpasteurized milk on that holiday in Switzerland but could never really get to the bottom of it. She was told it was like malaria, in the sense that it would reoccur, and she would never be free of it, which proved to be the case. She even contemplated going over to America at one point. She'd contacted a doctor there who was pioneering a cure, but Dad talked her out of that idea, for fear of getting conned by a quack. I think that's why he agreed to go on those cruises, because she suffered so badly at those other times.

My brother Cliff met and married Chris in 1968, the year before the Pub opened. Cliff knew Chris's Aunt Violet when he was chef at the Headland Hotel. Aunt Vi lived with her husband Gerald and ran their guest house on Henver road in the Summer. In Winter, Vi ran the dining room at the many banquets held at the Headland Hotel and when Chris had come down on holiday from her home in Catford, south west London, she'd introduced Cliff and Chris and they hit it off straightaway.

Banquets were the mainstay in the Winter for kitchen and dining room staff. With most hotels having closed for the Winter, it was the only work available to some and the two pounds and meal thrown in kept the wolf from the door for many, with full silver service waiting on staff being in most demand. They got the jobs by word of mouth normally and regular faces would work the circuit of hotels, including the Kilbirnie, the Bristol and even at the R.A.F camp at St. Mawgan. A favourite night to work, if you could get it, was on Burns night up at the camp where the Haggis would be heralded in, by a lone piper.

After getting married, Chris and Cliff took over the lease on Danesbury House up Fore street, a big house, to run as a B&B, just a few doors away from Frances and Alan's fruit and veg shop, the 'Fruit Basket', which they'd opened a couple of years before.

The Pub went from strength to strength. Locals loved it as they always got a warm welcome, whoever was behind the bar.

Holidaymakers loved it, once they'd stumbled across it, coming back day after day, or year after year in some cases, like the family from Liverpool who spent their three week shutdown from Ford's, spending every night in the Pub.

It looked as though you'd walked into someone's front room, when you walked into the main bar, with dolls and castanets, given to me by friends and family, brought back from holidays, displayed in the recessed glass fronted cupboard. A coal scuttle next to the open fire. Ornaments and bric a brac in abundance. The deep reds of the geraniums in the window boxes outside the long windows by the dart board, matched the red of the cushions Mum had made for the bench seating.

But that's what customers loved. The homeliness and warmth of a proper pub.

That's why it was so successful.

I loved living there.

All night long

I shoved open the old heavy front door of the Central Hotel, with some trepidation as I'd only been there a short while and everything was still strange. Meeting new people, learning the ropes as a receptionist and what was expected of me was a challenge, but one I knew I was going to love. My chambermaid days were, hopefully over.

Stepping from the brightness of the early morning sunshine into the cool darkness of the hotel foyer, took me a minute for my eyes to adjust. The area wasn't huge, but with its ebony panelling, said to be reclaimed from an old local Sea Captain's cabin framing the square hall with the long high backed bench seats each side covered in deep pile red velvet cushions, it made an imposing first impression.

There'd been an Inn on this site since 1755, so was infamous for its chequered past and tales of smugglers and pirates. The office come reception desk was straight ahead, with the shutters down until I unlocked it for the shift ahead. The door to the restaurant was to the left, just inside the front door, with the stairs to the right of the reception, just back a bit, hidden from view, around the corner. Something caught my eye and I instinctively glanced to my immediate right, through the patterned glass door into the Cocktail Bar.

'What the…..'

There were dim lights on behind the bar, the deep red velvet curtains on the windows overlooking Central Square were closed and with only a couple of table lamps giving additional limited illumination, it was difficult to see through the gloom and smoky haze. But I could make out Ray, the head barman behind the bar with the Hotel manager Mr Shortland propping up the end as usual, talking to a handful of men, sitting or standing around the bar with glasses in their hands in various states of emptiness.

Its seven-o-clock. In the morning!

Taken aback, I froze for a minute. Ray spotted me, saying something to Mr S. who then came out of the other door from the bar, nearest to the reception. I was still at the front door, not knowing quite what to do as this was a first for me, thinking I'd stumbled on some secret society that has those funny handshakes!

'Close the door over, would you Denise,' he said quite nonchalantly. *'Don't want any prying eyes.'*

Handing me the key to the office and now a little closer, he looked dishevelled, with his shirt top button undone and tie askew, he didn't look his normal immaculate self and offering no explanation, he shot back into the bar.

I opened the reception, pulled up the shutter, pottered about, getting sorted for the busy day ahead. I was trying not to be noticed, which was a bit difficult considering the reception hatchway was so big, I couldn't fail to be seen. But I was doing my best to nonchalantly glance up from time to time, in a bid to spot any familiar faces who had been drinking all night, as they gradually sidled their way out of the bar and skedaddled through the front door.

Well, I thought, *wait til I tell Mum about this!*

Then I thought better of it, because if she thought there were any kind of shenanigans going on, she might have made me leave.

After the busy Christmas I'd had working at the Bristol and desperate for a change, I was thrilled when I got the job of Receptionist at Easter. It wasn't just a Summer job, it was permanent, quite a rarity, as the Central was one of only a handful of places that stayed open all year and wasn't mothballed for the Winter. I was one of only two receptionists and the shifts were 7-2.30 and 2-9.30.

We crossed paths for half hour at 2 o-clock for a handover and to update the evening receptionist on any ongoing issue. It was six days a week, so when one of us had our day off, Mrs Shortland the manageress covered the other shift.

Mr and Mrs Roy Edwards owned the Central, but they lived at their other hotel, The Tides Reach in Salcombe, Devon. Mr Edwards was well known around Newquay, having been a keen rugby player, in his time, for the Hornets, who based their headquarters at the Central, when he played for them.

It was Mr and Mrs Ken Shortland, who managed the Central for them, who lived on site and who I reported to on a day to day basis. They had a flat right at the far end of the hotel on the first floor and that is where I would normally pick up the key on the morning shift. They'd leave it on the window ledge outside their flat door, which was down a long corridor, way out of sight of any guests.

I started at the Central in April 1969. I was 17.

It soon became clear that I wasn't just a receptionist but expected to do a bit of everything, but I didn't mind as keeping busy made the days go faster and I could wear my own clothes, no black uniform, so that was a bonus.

The other receptionist, some years older than me, was married to an R.A.F pilot stationed at St. Mawgan and had been at the Central a while. She was nice enough but seemed to take a little too much pleasure in pointing out any mistakes I made. Good job our paths only crossed for a short time each day and as time wore on and I got more experienced, I gave her less opportunity to gloat at any shortcomings.

The reception office was square, about the same size as the entrance hall, but being in the centre of the building, had no windows. When the large shutter was open, there was a ledge for guests and customers to lean on while talking to us, so we had to keep everywhere tidy. Looking into the office, to the right, was a wall of wine racks housing a good selection of wines such as Blue Nun, Pouilly-Fuisse and Mateus Rose.

Just behind this was a door to the cupboard under the stairs which housed the wall safe. At the back was a frosted glass door which led straight into the kitchen but was obscured by the massive rich dark wood floor to ceiling bureau that sat against the wall on the left, acting as a partial room divider. When Mrs

Shortland was sitting behind it, dealing with the business of the day, she couldn't be seen.

That meant there were some sticky moments when a staff member would come to the reception desk to ask me something or to have a moan.

'Do you know what she's got me doing now, the stupid old bat...'

'Nooooo', I said loudly, trying to shut up the ginger haired Scots barman from the Saddle bar, who was always a bit loud and had a lot to say and not always complimentary about the management.

Knowing from past encounters that he was about to say something uncomplimentary about Mrs S, I waved my arms frantically at him, pointing behind me.

'What's that girlfriend of yours up to now?' I added, trying to deflect the inevitable.

He looked at me as though I had two heads, before it dawned on him that Mrs S must be sitting behind the bureau.

Once all the staff had encountered my over the top dramatic gestures once, a quick nod or a shake of my head before they spoke would tell them whether she was in situ or not. Hairy moments and potential sackings avoided.

To the left of the office, this side of the bureau, was the small hatch into the restaurant where Violet the Cornish waitress would stand and chat to me when custom was slow.

The hotel had fifteen bedrooms of different sizes. It had three bars, the Cocktail, Saddle Bar and Gig bar on the end and together with the busy restaurant, which was popular with both guests and non-residents, the hotel had a thriving trade.

Of course, licensing hours were stricter back then, none of this all day opening, so the restaurant closed at 2 p.m. each day. and the bars closed at 3 p.m., both re-opening again at 6 p.m. and the many staff that worked in the kitchen, restaurant, bars and upstairs rooms, would go home or to their small rooms in the eaves of the hotel, or to the staff house in Golf Terrace off Tower road which the hotel owned. To have a well-earned rest for a few hours before returning for the evening shift.

As most guests would be out for the day, the afternoons would be a few hours of relative peace and quiet with no-one else around, but me, before the onslaught of the evening rush.

Mr and Mrs S had distinct roles within the hotel. It varied sometimes, but primarily she would be on duty during the day, dealing with any arising issues and handling all the bookings for the hotel. He was very much the convivial host, occasionally at lunchtime but he came into his own of an evening, positioning himself at the end of the Cocktail Bar, chatting to guests and locals alike, making them feel welcome.

So, my dealings were mainly with Mrs S, but they were both good to work for and were patient with me when I first started, which they needed to be. Behind the bureau in reception, was the telephone and switchboard, if you can call it that, because it only had four extensions which connected to their flat, the bar, restaurant and kitchen. There were no phones in the guest rooms. Mr S had shown me how to use it.

Simple I thought, it was up, down, left, or right. What could possibly go wrong. Mr Ravillious, the local journalist would probably tell you otherwise as when he phoned one day to speak to Mr S, I cut him off four times.

In the end Mr S came all the way down to reception from his flat to phone him back. Sacked, I thought, but no, he was very understanding, and I soon got the hang of it.

In Summer, the front door would be open wide and I'd sit and daydream, as I watched the hordes of chattering holidaymakers pass by, wondering where they were from or what they did. My view consisted of a row of shops opposite, including Whitehouse the Jewellers, the Central Meat company and the Millbay laundry on the corner.

Mum must have sent a lot of linen to be cleaned at one time, because she 'acquired' one of their huge laundry baskets, which now resides in my garage. Still going strong over fifty years later. Another great storage item that has accompanied me on our house moves.

With no computers back then to manage the hotel, everything was recorded into a huge ledger which was kept on the desk. It was our bible. Mrs S would enter the hotel bookings as they came in, so we'd know exactly who was expected on any given day. My primary role as a hotel receptionist involved cheerily booking the guests in on their arrival, taking their car registration as there was sometimes a free for all when it came to parking out front the hotel. Despite big signs saying residents only, it was obvious that some people couldn't read.

Plus, as I was usually the only member of staff around in the afternoon, I'd double up as hotel porter sometimes carrying bulging suitcases up to the rooms before offering guests a tray of tea to help them settle in. I'd be making it in the kitchen and nearly jump out of my skin, when Mrs S, who was a large lady but surprisingly light on her feet would sometimes suddenly appear beside me.

She'd come down from their flat to make Mr S his favourite cheese on toast and because there was a flight of stairs from the first floor going straight into the kitchen, I wouldn't know she was there. I think she did it on purpose to see what I was up to.

There wasn't very often any trouble in the Central. But when there was, Big Dave from the Vic Bars behind the Central, could always be called upon to lend a hand and help to escort any undesirables from the premises. Despite the Central being in direct competition with other nearby pubs, like the Sailors, the Vic Bars and the Newquay Arms, in vying for customers, there was a camaraderie between them all.

If any of them ran out of beer, they'd borrow a barrel until the next delivery. Likewise, with bottles of spirits or wine. To be honest, the town was heaving back then, so there was more than enough thirsty and hungry customers to go around.

After we'd left the Bristol Hotel and I'd started work in the Central, Pat rented a bedsit up Fore street, almost opposite Danesbury, where Cliff and Chris lived.

He was working up at R.A.F St. Mawgan in the dining room as a waiter, so bought a moped to get there and back. No helmet required.

His bedsit looked over Fore street, but at the back, was the most spectacular, panoramic sea view overlooking the harbour and beyond. Sad to say, we took that view for granted at the time.

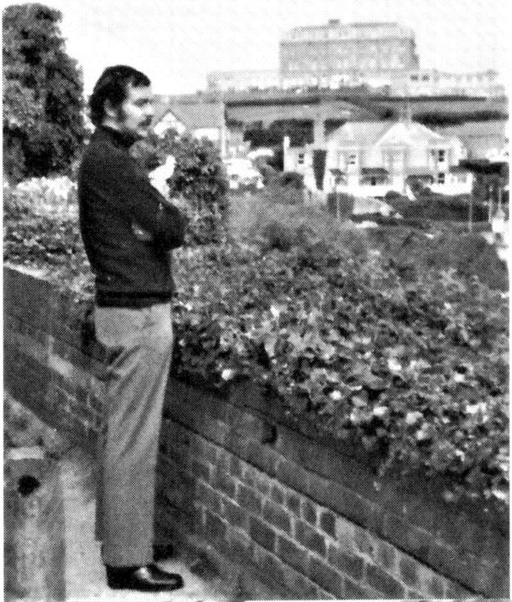

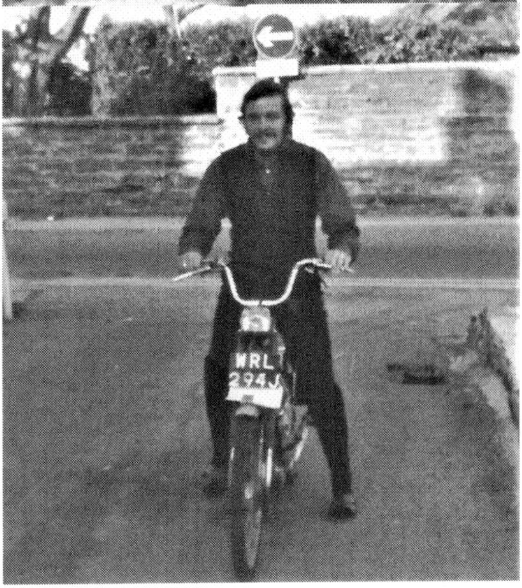
WRL
294J

The kitchen in the Central was huge. With a bank of ovens in an L shape, multiple gas rings in the centre, extensive storeroom, sinks, grills, cooking equipment, cutlery, and china galore with a huge, well used stainless steel stock pot permanently simmering away. It was impressive.

Bob the chef was painfully thin. It made me wonder if he was actually eating his own food. The restaurant had a table d'hote menu for guests staying with us on a Dinner, Bed and Breakfast basis, plus an A la carte menu, which included Steak Diane, Lobster Thermidor and Crepe Suzette flambéed at the table by George, the tall Tommy Cooper look alike, head waiter.

The resident waitress, Violet, a true Cornishwoman, resembled a gypsy with her jet-black hair and rugged tanned face. I loved Violet. A lot older than me, but with her infectious laugh, broad Cornish accent, sunny nature, and permanent smile, she was a joy to be around. She lived in a cottage just around the corner in Chapel Hill and would come in early before evening service to make the Melba toast, which I'd never seen made before, so was fascinated.

She'd grill both sides of a slice of bread, after first removing the crusts, then carefully slice right through the middle with a sharp knife, then put the untoasted sides back under the grill. Now so thin, the slices curled up and crisped, ready to serve with Pate that evening. If I were filling the kettle to make tea while she was doing that and let the tap run, she'd have to dive for the loo. Seeing running water always did that to her.

Proper Cornish, *'I'll do that dreckly'* or *'Zackly'* were her usual sayings.

Lobster Thermidor had to be pre-ordered, you couldn't just walk in and order it off the menu, as the lobsters needed to be fresh. One quiet afternoon, I'd gone into the kitchen to make tea and went over to the back door to close it as someone had left it open, only to find Lobsters crawling all over the floor. When they were required, the local fisherman would come in through the back gate and with no-one around pop them onto the draining board by the sink just inside the door, ready for the chef when he came back on duty. Still alive, these pesky things had gone walkabout and fallen onto the floor.

There was no way I was going anywhere near them, so I left them there crawling around. What hadn't crossed my mind until I saw it happening that evening, was how they were cooked. I'll never forget the squeals they made when dropped into a huge pot of boiling water, turning from black to vivid red in the process. Apparently its done that way to kill any toxins.

But all I could think about was the fact that I'd turn bright red as well if I'd been dropped into boiling water.

Seeing and hearing that was enough to put you off Lobster for life.

All creatures great and (not so) small

I didn't get completely away from chambermaid duties. If necessary, I'd have to occasionally give guests their early morning wake-up call and tray of tea. Reminiscent of my time at the Minerva, I'd knock on the door, shouting *'Morning Tea,'* and not waiting for an answer just barge in. Well I was only seventeen and still pretty naïve, despite seeing some of the things I'd already been privy to.

Several times, if it had been a warm night, I'd catch young couples still fast asleep, completely naked with not even a sheet still on the bed to give any cover to their intimate parts. I'd quietly deposit the tray on the dressing table, trying not to look and bang the door as I went out, shouting morning tea, to try and arouse them whilst I crept away, red faced.

'Bottle of Blue Nun please,' George the Head waiter said, slapping the docket down onto the spike by the hatch, which was in-between the restaurant and reception. Evening dinner service was in full swing, the restaurant was busy, and I could hear the swing doors between the kitchen and the dining room going twenty to the dozen as the waiting staff rushed through with food orders.

The chef barked orders to the Sous chef, who in turn barked orders to the Commis chef and they all barked orders at the poor Kitchen porter who wasn't washing the pots quick enough, in their opinion. Who, in my opinion, always smelt of booze, so I'd give him a wide birth. There would be shouting and swearing and tempers flaring, dishes dropped. It could be bedlam. I couldn't understand what made chefs so cranky and the language, well that was choice.

But I'd grown up with colourful language, not from Mum or Dad, as their worst was bugger, bloody 'ell or blinking 'eck. No, I learnt a whole raft of new swear words from my brother who was a chef at the Trelawney Hotel, down Edgcumbe Avenue at the time.

If I got up to go to the loo in the middle of the night or down to the kitchen and passed Cliff's bedroom, he'd be having a full-scale humdinger of a row with someone in his sleep. He'd be calling them all the names under the sun and swearing like a trooper, clear as a bell.

Come the morning he didn't know what we were talking about, had no recollection. I wondered if he wanted to rant and rave at someone but kept it all inside and then it came out in his sleep. But having seen other cantankerous chefs, thought better of that and realised that he must have really had a right old go at some poor sod in his kitchen, during dinner service.

Everything a customer ordered in the Central's dining room, whether it be food or drink was written on a docket and then put on the spike and then it was my responsibility to start a bill for each table. If they ordered additional food or drinks, another docket would be made out until they'd finished their meal and I'd make up the final bill. Ray the head barman made sure the wine racks were fully stocked each day and if the customers wanted drinks from the bar, George, in his dinner suit and dickie bow and despite his tall frame, would nimbly rush past the reception with his silver tray and the next minute come back the other way, skilfully carrying it, usually fully laden, not a drop spilt.

If the customers were guests of the hotel, the cost would either already be included in their room cost or if they'd had something extra off the A la Carte menu, it would be added to the ledger for their room number. For all other guests, they paid at the table and the monies passed through to me. Cash was king as cheques could only be guaranteed up to £30 with the cheque guarantee card that had not long been introduced.

The Central did take some cheques over that amount particularly for payment of rooms where they had the customers names and addresses, but still occasionally a cheque would come back from the Bank stating 'Refer to Drawer', meaning we'd have to get back in touch with the customer for payment. With the Banking process being so slow, it could take about 12 days for them to return a cheque to us. The Central banked with Lloyds, which was just opposite at the bottom of Crantock street, next to the Central Arcade. Mrs S would take the takings over daily or keep them in the safe over the weekend.

As the Summer wore on, and things got hectic, nerves more frayed and endless days of work, work, work, I came to realise that the Central's cocktail bar had become a refuge for some locals and that all night boozy session I'd witnessed, started to become a regular fixture and turned into a card school as well.

Not every night, I don't think anyone had the stamina to keep up with that, but it didn't surprise me anymore if they were all still in the bar when I arrived for work in the morning. I think they all gravitated towards it, because it was somewhere where they could come and know there would be someone else in the same hectic Summer bubble and understood and could lend a sympathetic ear.

It was mainly a mix of hoteliers and business owners, the movers, and shakers of the town. Amongst them was Tony Lake, an ex-policeman, turned Insurance man. He was always pleasant and polite. Frank Manning with his long blond hair, who owned the Cabaret Club on the corner of Edgcumbe avenue and was brother to Bernard Manning, the comedian. Mr Hook, who owned the Harbour hotel, who scared me to death with his hooked hand. He wasn't very pleasant.

But most of them were nice and waved or said hello and had a little chat, but then there was the shady car dealer with dirty fingernails and various other hangers on, all desperately striving to be in with the town's elite. Ageing Jack the lads that didn't seem to want to grow up, mainly harmless, but seemingly wanting to prove that they still had what it took, with the ladies. Several made me feel uncomfortable and I'd be so thankful that the reception desk acted as a protective barrier against their smarmy smiles and lecherous leers.

Mr S always treated me with respect and courtesy, but I soon realised that his love and consumption of whisky and his chain smoking of cigarettes did make him twitch and shake so badly before that first tipple. It would be a nightmare trying to hand him anything. We'd both get so embarrassed. Some regulars would only come in at lunchtime, like Mr Whitehouse and Sheila from the Jewellery shop opposite. Not sure why no-one referred to them as Mr and Mrs Whitehouse, but it was always Mr Whitehouse and Sheila. She'd worked at the Victoria Hotel, at the same time as my Pat.

The Edwards would occasionally visit from Salcombe to see how things were going and there would be a buzz about the place in anticipation of their arrival with everyone on their best behaviour. That meant Mr S would need to be around during the day, which wasn't his natural habitat, so he was usually a nervous shaking wreck. Roy Edwards was a tall imposing figure and the bar was always busy when he was around as he caught up with old friends.

Not sure if he knew about those all-night sessions, but if he did, he turned a blind eye, because they carried on, but not while he was visiting. I couldn't possibly tell you who else frequented the Cocktail Bar but let's just say that most of the key hotel and business owners of the town, whose names you'd hear frequently were customers at one time or another. People like Luxon who owned the Headland; John King, the Red Lion; Norman Anstiss, the Sailors; Barlow, the Kilbirnie; Stuart Young, the Bristol; Boydens, the Victoria; Stan

Pickles, the Fistral Bay; Carlton, the Bredon Court; Pascoe, the Atlantic; Tangye, the Glendorgal; Armstrong the Edgcumbe; Derrick Jones from Trevelgue and many more whom I'm sure would have visited the Central at some time or another as it became the go to watering hole for local business people.

We had celebrities coming into the restaurant and bar as well. Terence Alexander, the actor, who had a typical British accent and who would go on to star in the television series Bergerac in the 1990's, came in one day and he spoke exactly the same as on the tele. That same posh voice.

I was supposed to finish the evening shift at 9.30 p.m., but when I finished depended on how long diners lingered in the restaurant. If there was no sign of a table making a move after they'd finished a meal, George would subtlety turn some of the lights off in the dining room.

Violet would start setting the tables for breakfast and if that didn't work, they'd go and get their coats and bags and stand waiting by the door through to the kitchen. I'd then close the reception and head home. In the height of Summer, it would still be light, with loads of people around, but in the depths of Winter, it was pitch black and hardly a soul around, but I was so used to the long walk home, it didn't worry me.

All was going well that first Summer. I was familiar with the routine as everything became second nature. Which was a good job as sometimes I was still a little dozy from the early start, when I arrived in the morning. I was holding my own, getting used to the lobsters in the kitchen and the lechers in the bar, but something else was about to rock my world and not in a good way.

The usual all-night session was on its last legs in the bar, with only a few stragglers left, when I unlocked the office door one morning and went to walk in. I knew I'd trodden on something disgusting when it popped and crunched loudly as my foot slid across the floor, splattering beneath my wooden Dr Scholl's. I went cold.

It was the scurrying noises from within though, that momentarily galvanised me to the spot before I lunged forward and banged on the light switch. The ancient yellowing strip light flickered, briefly illuminating what looked like a suspended moving carpet. As the light finally sprang fully to life, panic gripped me as I faced the full horror. Sweaty and nauseous, gagging for air, I spun around slamming the door behind me, my screams bouncing off the walls of the hotel foyer!

'Aaaaagghhhhhhhhhh'

Mr S, no doubt buoyed by the amount of whisky he'd consumed all night and having found, for a change, that it was *me* shaking and distressed and only able to point dumbstruck at the office, gallantly came to my rescue and flung open the door before I had time to stammer out 'Cockrrrrr...oaches!'

He stood in the doorway looking perplexed and when I'd plucked up the courage, peeped in after him, amazed to find that the previous mass of disgustingly huge armour-plated non-paying guests that had frightened me senseless had all but disappeared. Only a few remained, clinging on to the new dart board propped up against the bureau.

'There were thousands,' I said emphatically, but his sceptical look told me he wasn't convinced.

The pest control man was duly called, very matter of fact, as if it was an everyday occurrence. I had to carry on working in the office, under much duress, having become even more of a nervous trembling wreck.

Still having to smile sweetly to the guests, keeping secret the teeny weenie fact that their holiday hideaway was also inhabited with obnoxious beasties. My skin crawled for days as my imagination ran riot and I visualised cockroaches lurking in every conceivable corner and when it came to putting money in the safe under the stairs, well that was one dark crevice I wasn't going to venture into, so I tried to leave that to Mrs S. But it taught me to be vigilant and let's just say that Fred, the pest control man became a good friend.

Mr Edwards would always visit before Christmas and he'd give me fifty pounds bonus every year, which I thought was marvellous.

Despite all my experiences with creepy crawlies and creatures of all persuasion, many more of which I was to encounter during that summer, I concluded that I disliked them all. But if I was forced to choose my preferred 'beastie', it would probably be the multi legged variety.

Unlike some of the two-legged versions that frequented that Cocktail bar, at least I didn't have to endure them trying to chat me up *as well* as giving me the creeps!

The 'goings-on'

The stories of *'goings on,'* in the Summer were endless. Snippets overheard, rumours passed on, full blown scandals exposed or tales from personal experience. They were all there. You couldn't make them up. Real life was much more interesting than fiction. Nothing shocked in the end….

'Can you do me washing?' he said as he sidled up beside me. I was walking past the dentist surgery on East street opposite Shrimptons' the Jewellers. Trevor Shrimpton was a mate of Frances and Alan.

'What?' I said turning to look at him. Mum always told me off for saying *'what'* instead of pardon.

'Me washing, I've got no-one to do me washing, you must have a machine at home, would your Mum do it for me?'

I'd seen him around town a few times. He'd probably seen me in my school uniform, knew I was local.

'No, sorry,' I said, just about to give him an excuse, when he marched off, a man with a mission. I saw him sidle up to another girl a hundred yards ahead.

That was the nature of things, you soon got to recognise who the workers were as opposed to holidaymakers, because you'd see them around week after week, so you'd know they weren't on their two week summer holiday.

But they wouldn't necessarily be working for a living. It's a miracle that the hotels made any money. When the out of towners started their hotel jobs at the beginning of a season, they landed on their feet with three meals a day and living accommodation that would either be in separate staff houses close by or staff rooms in the hotel accessed by a separate entrance. Usually away from prying eyes of the hotel management. Easy to sneak someone in and I don't mean just girls. As the season went on, they'd talk to mates back home, no doubt boasting about the incredible time they were having. Sex, surfing, and sunbathing. How could their mates resist?

'Come down,' they'd say. *'I'll put you up.'*

There it was, an open invitation for them to bunk in with their mates in the staff quarters all over town, sharing beds, sleeping on floors, whatever it took. And as for feeding them, well buying the hotel chef a few pints now and again, would guarantee they'd finish their shift with a full English breakfast or a roast beef dinner plated up, cloth over ready to take to the mate waiting in their staff room. Accommodation and food sorted. All for free. Hotel owners oblivious or too busy to worry.

So, what with locals, holidaymakers, hotel workers and then all their mates, the town heaved to bursting and questions like *'will you do me washing'* was just one of many a strange request.

Then there was the constant movement of staff between hotels.

Especially if you were good at what you did, such as being a silver-service waiter. Someone who could carry more than two plates at a time was always in demand. Few and far between.

Rows with management or arguments with other staff would prompt someone to walk out mid-shift sometimes. Serving breakfast in the Tolcarne hotel for instance and then dinner in the Savoia, having moved their possessions in the afternoon, to yet another staff room, was a common occurrence.

Of course, not all the 'waiters' were bonafide waiters, they just said that to get a job, only to be found out in the course of a busy service….

'What d'ya mean you've taken the gravy in, its sitting right there in those jugs,' chef said.

'Chef, we've already taken it in,' replied the waiter.

Chef walked over to the sauceboats, stuck his finger in one and tasted.

'What the hell have you done?' he said looking daggers at the young waiters sheepishly standing around the kitchen, then peaked through the swing doors into the guests dining room. The coach party of pensioners were all tucking into their roast beef dinner. He could see gravy boats on the tables.

'You've given them the chocolate sauce, instead of gravy, you morons, that was for the pudding,' chef shouted, incandescent with rage.

Knives got lashed, pots got thrown and custard quickly made to go with the chocolate pudding.

The waiters dreaded going back into the dining room.

But they needn't have worried. All the plates came back clean. Not a drop of chocolate sauce left over. I couldn't possibly tell you in which hotel this happened but suffice to say it's knocked down now, with flats in its place!

Then there were the fights, scuffles and punch ups....

'I see there was another fight outside the Sailors again last night,' Dad said as he came in from doing the weekly shop at Chaffins, having heard all about it from the lad who helped him load up the car. There had already been one the previous week between Scousers and the Irish. That was a real humdinger.

'Yes,' Dad carried on. *'It got really nasty apparently. Liverpool and Irish hotel workers versus rockers from St. Austell.'*

The Scousers and Irish had obviously patched up their differences, from the week before and joined forces.

'You mind you stay away from those hotel workers,' Mum piped in, looking at me, with a look that gave away the sudden nasty taste in her mouth.

'They're nothing but trouble,' she added. No mention of the part the Cornish rockers had played in the brawl.

Then there was the usual throwing out of undesirables or drunks from every establishment in town. That was normal, everyday, with the Sailors and Vic Bars being the most notorious.

You argued at your peril with Norman from the Sailors or Big Dave from the Vic Bars.

'He was drunk on Pernod, lost his shoe, didn't know what he was doing or where he was, he was in a right state,' I could hear a lad telling his mate, as I was walking behind them down the tramlines.

'Started rummaging around under tables, looking for his shoe, touching up girl's legs in the process, knocking drinks everywhere, causing mayhem apparently and just as Norman went to throw him out of the Sailors, he spewed up all over the floor.'

Then there was just the plain outrageous...

'What the effing ell ave ya done?' said the waiter to his non-paying room guest, that had come down from Liverpool, to bunk in with him. Lost for words, the waiter held up two cut off legs from his waiter's dress trousers, not quite believing what he was seeing.

'I didn't have any shorts, la,' his mate said parading around the room in the cut off waiter's trousers now looking less like Bermuda shorts than you could imagine. But he was still dead pleased with himself, despite his 'shorts' being jet black with a satin stripe down the side.

Then there was the sad...

'Another poor sod's gone over the cliff,' Dad said, having heard it from a local in the bar at lunchtime. The cliffs that were the backdrop to most of the beaches were precipitous and had little or no protection to stop someone falling over the edge, especially if they were drunk or got disorientated and lost their bearings.

This time, it had happened at the back of the shops on Cliff road and a lad had gone right over the edge onto the Great Western Beach. Killed instantly. It wasn't clear what he'd been doing there but this kind of tragedy happened a few times over the years.

Then there was plain revenge...

An Italian waitress in a big hotel up Tower road which shall be nameless, had enough of getting shouted at, harassed, and bullied by the patisserie chef, week after week. He had a taste for profiteroles and after he'd made them for the guest's sweet trolley each day would stash a plateful in the fridge for himself to enjoy after evening dinner service. Little did he know that one day she'd laced them with laxative.

He wasn't seen for a week.

A guest in the same hotel asked for a hard-boiled egg for his breakfast, only to be given a soft-boiled egg. He sent it back. Three times. Until he got so frustrated, he stormed into the kitchen and threw the egg at the breakfast chef, who ended up with runny yolk all over his bald head.

There were the staff who couldn't stand to sleep in the staff quarters of the Victoria hotel, convinced there were ghosts roaming the corridors. The Victoria had been used as a hospital in the second world war with the basement, where the staff quarters were situated, used as the morgue. There were tales of staff thinking they felt someone getting into bed with them on occasion, only to find nobody there.

Either ghosts or they'd consumed too many pints of Guinness.

There were the guests running off without paying, which was a result of mainly B & B's taking in guests 'on spec', not knowing the name and address they'd been given was false.

Lastly there was the 'soiled sheet syndrome'. When you went into a room to change the sheets after the guests had left, you never knew what state the bedding would be in. Usually okay, but sometimes you really didn't want to dawdle trying to investigate what exactly that stain on the bottom sheet was. You just whipped it off the bed, bundled it up, threw it out in the corridor to be collected, shivered and promptly washed your hands.

Should that stain be found during the week while the guests were still with you, you'd change the bedding and put a plastic sheet underneath, just to be safe, to protect the mattress.

I think all hotels and B&B's must have had a supply of those plastic sheets.

Somebody must have been cashing in!

Liverpool here I come

'*Don't look anyone straight in the eye,*' he told me, as we looked around for a taxi.

We'd arrived at Lime street station, Liverpool, after an arduous trip from Newquay. I thought the train journey was never going to end. It was cold and grey. It was October and I'd normally be going up to London with Mum and Dad, but here I was, with Pat, my boyfriend of nine months.

'*And don't talk,*' he added, '*Otherwise, they'll know you're a Woolyback.*'

'*What's a Woolyback?*' I asked.

'*Someone not from Liverpool,*' he said.

He wasn't purposely trying to scare me, just wanted me to know a few rules of Scouse land. A city that doesn't suffer fools easily, so an out of towner could be taken advantage of quite easily, by those disreputable morons that inhabit *every* big city. This was my first trip to Liverpool to meet his family. This shy, reserved Southerner, itching to venture out of sleepy old Cornwall and experience a big city as an adult. Mum hadn't been at all pleased when I'd told her about the trip.

'*You're going where on holiday?*' she quizzed.

'*Liverpool,*' I repeated, even though I knew she'd heard me the first time. Why anyone who lived in beautiful Cornwall, would want to travel up into what she considered the bleak, cold and unwelcoming landscape of the North of England, was beyond her. My future hubby was taking me to meet in laws for the first time, so I was somewhat apprehensive as well as travel weary after the endless, ten-hour, four change, train journey.

But I was smitten as soon as I stepped on to the station platform. The bracing wind from the Mersey whistled up through the historic streets, momentarily stopping us in our tracks. Waiting to greet us was the backside of the stunning 19th century St. Georges Hall, standing proud and magnificent. They built it back to front apparently.

The helter-skelter of traffic and hustle and bustle on the streets was a far cry from the sleepy Cornish town I was used to in the Winter, where walking was the mode of transport and the sighting of a bus or taxi, just a rumour. It was late and we were tired, by the time we arrived at Pat's family house in Goodwood street, just down from Scotland Road, or Scottie as it's known.

Pat's Mum wasn't home from her evening cleaning job in the Cooper's buildings, but she'd left two bowls of Scouse thickening up slowly in the oven. It smelt divine. A bit like stew, but so, so much better. Beef with a little lamb thrown in, carrots, onions and loads of potatoes that soften and break up with the slow cooking, making it really thick, then all put into bowls in the oven to form a skin on top, that wraps in all the flavour. So that when you delve in and taste that first mouthful, it's comfort food in abundance. She'd left a plateful of buttered barm cakes, covered on the table.

We devoured the lot.

I was given the spare double bedroom and Pat slept on the sofa. Tired out, but couldn't sleep with excitement, I heard Pat's Dad, Chick, as everyone called him, don't think anyone knew why, as he came in from the Brittania Pub, cursing as he fell up the stairs. I slept like a log after that.

Next day, I was made to feel like the Queen. I was positioned in the living room, given copious cups of tea while a never-ending stream of relations came to have a nosey at Pat's new girlfriend and there were loads. Such a big family.

There was no kissing or hugging, they aren't that sort of family. No touchy feely, but they'd do anything for you, that was a given, without the need to show affection. Not like my Mum, who had to be kissed practically every time you left the room and she'd remind you if you forgot. I got such a warm welcome, even if I was a Woolyback and with Scousers renowned for loving their food, I had a chip butty thrust in my hand before I'd got my coat off on many occasion during my stay.

With conversations at breakneck speed, constant banter and everyone talking at once, nineteen to the dozen, in that unmistakeable accent, I needed an interpreter. I had no chance of getting a word in edgeways, which suited me fine. There were never any awkward silences in their house.

Although I'd listened avidly to Pat's stories, I knew little about the city. We did the rounds of sights to see, taking the ferry across the Mersey to New Brighton and then on to Chester Zoo and that river view of the

World-famous Liverpool waterfront… breath taking. I'd thought the 'Three Graces' were a pop group until it was pointed out that these were the iconic Royal Liver, Cunard and Port of Liverpool buildings dominating the Pier Head.

    I had a must-see tour of the Gents toilets in the Philharmonic pub; this marbled wonder being the only Grade 2 listed toilets in the country. Then there were the two Cathedrals, the Beatles hang outs, the Museums, the Walker Art gallery……the sights were endless. Captivating this Cornish Pixie whose main excitement in life thus far, had been watching high tide.

From the Three graces to Greaty market, from St. Georges Hall to George Henry Lees, from the Legs of Man Pub to Mann Island, I was smitten.

Buildings steeped in history. Streets with hidden secrets, I'd sit spellbound for hours, captivated by the stories his family loved to tell about working on the docks or the fruit market or of the Cunard Yanks. So called, because they were the crew who worked on the transatlantic shipping routes from Liverpool to New York from the 1940's through to the 1960's. Bringing back rock and roll and soul and blues music as well as American fashion to the city. Scousers are great story tellers.

But the highlight of the trip was to be the Saturday night out at St. Sylvester's social club opposite the church of the same name. I'd gone into the city centre that day to buy a new skirt, top and coat and was looking forward to a lively night. I'd window shopped in Lucinda Byre an expensive lady's shop, down the bottom of Bold street and marvelled at the grandeur of George Henry Lees.

Quite how lively that night was going to be I hadn't anticipated. The place was packed. Trestle tables and chairs filled to capacity, laden to near collapse with glasses galore, bottles of ale and foil parcels brought from home full of bacon ribs, pork ribs, sandwiches, drumsticks and pork pies, all to be enjoyed later in the evening.

Large families gathered around tables, jostling for position. The noise was near deafening what with all the chatter and the live music. As the evening wore on and with a lot more ale being consumed by all, a fight suddenly broke out. Chairs got lashed, punches were thrown and for one innocent moment I thought that was it, but with such large families and everybody knowing each other or related, it seemed like the whole place joined in.

'*Leave our Billy alone,*' someone would shout, as they ran off to join the fray. The women were either trying to prize people apart or joining in themselves and I was suddenly left on my own.

Nothing for it, but to dive under the table. Didn't want my new clothes getting spoiled. In the intervening fifty years since that first visit, Liverpool has had its fair share of challenges, but you couldn't find a better example of the saying '*Pick yourself up, dust yourself off and start all over again*'.

It is now a vibrant, cosmopolitan city, full of humour, style, history, and culture… and as for me? Well I'm now an adopted Scouser, even if I still can't keep up with the break-neck speed conversations!

I found out that the word Scouse comes from the Vikings. It seems that when they invaded Britain, they brought with them a dish called 'Lobscouse', meaning spoon meat. Sailors called it Loblolly. It was easy to prepare in the one pot and eat at sea. Vikings are renowned for being, confident, outgoing and an adventurous nation, having great feasts with vast tables overflowing with food and drink, with hospitality in abundance. They must have left a few Vikings behind, because that's Scousers all over.

But even though I know where the word comes from, for me, Scouse will always have originated in my future mother-in-law's kitchen.

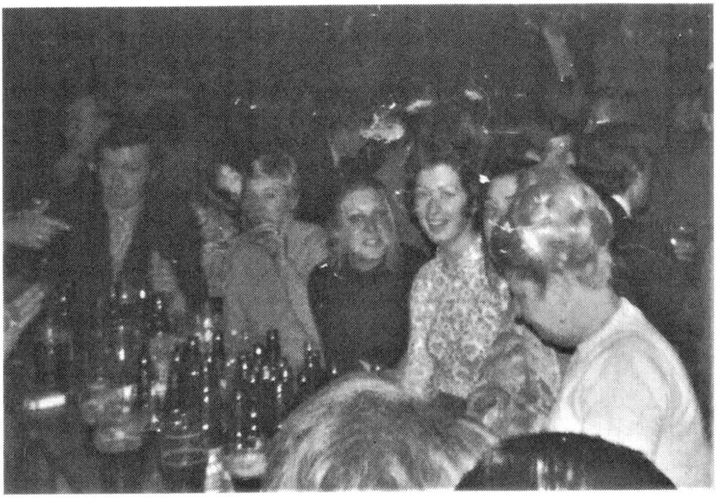

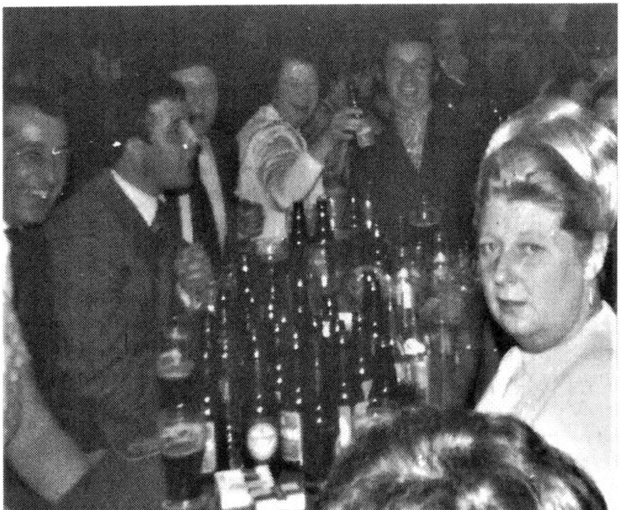

The Bust Up

'Don't talk to her like that,' Pat snapped at my Mum, as he stopped wiping the beer mug in his hand.

'Uh-oh', I thought, here comes trouble.

There was no love lost between the two of them and it was becoming more apparent by the day. We were in the restaurant bar of Treninnick Tavern, Mum and Dad's Pub on a busy Summer evening. Pat was now working there as a barman. I was still working at the Central, but we'd moved into the large front bedroom above the restaurant bar at the Tavern at the beginning of that Summer. So, they couldn't avoid each other. Mum had never taken to him.

'He'll have a girl in every port you know,' she'd say, whenever she thought I would listen. But it fell on deaf ears. Not only had Pat been in the Merchant Navy, but he was from Liverpool, one of those dastardly Northerners, in her words, and to cap it all, he was a hotel worker, when we'd met. She'd warned me off those many a time. Triple whammy!

Despite her protestations, Patrick Jones and I got married on 2nd October 1971, with the lovely Ron Doyle taking our wedding photos. We were going to get married in Truro registry office, so we'd planned for that and Mum had made me a lovely light beige velvet suit for the occasion. A big white wedding in a church had never been my dream. Too much attention for my liking.

But Pat's Mum had other ideas, because coming from a good Catholic family, she wanted us to get married in front of a priest, so after a bit or wrangling we duly obeyed. The suit stayed though, as weddings were a bit more avant-garde then with all kinds of ensembles sashaying their way down the aisles.

With me having been brought up as Church of England, I had to go for 'lessons' with Father Maggs, before we could get married in the Most Holy Trinity Catholic church on Tower Road. That's when he told me, seriously, but with a smile on his face, that I was a heathen in the eyes of the Catholic church as I had never been christened.

It was only a small affair, with Frank Jones, Pat's mate, another Scouser, as best man, a handful of friends and family with Pat's Dad and his teenage brother Frankie, the only ones making it down from Liverpool.

Don't know where Pat's Mum got Frankie's suit from, but the trousers reached up to under his armpits and when he put the jacket on, it looked like it still had the hanger in it. The black shirt about four sizes too big and white kipper tie completed his outfit. But Frankie didn't care, didn't worry about the hilarity it caused, he just loved being there.

There were only twelve of us at the wedding breakfast, which Mum had put together and consisted of, yes you guessed it, a ham salad. She loved a ham salad, my Mum.

It was just family, as well as Margaret, Mum's lifelong friend from when she grew up in Hackney, London and her husband Ted, who was in the leather trade. Margaret was always so well turned out, sporting lovely handbags and gloves.

The evening 'bit of a do' for friends and family with Mum letting her hair down after a few sherries and twisting away to Chubby Checker, was a much livelier affair.

With all Pat's mates who were living in Newquay, able to enjoy it with us. Frank and Kath Jones, Dave and Jackie Perkins, John and Viv Ash, Nick and Lyn Disley and Brian Dirkin.

My school mates were all away at College or University by then and I'd lost touch with most of them

We spent our honeymoon back in Liverpool, travelling there with his Dad and brother a day or two after the wedding. Along with Dave Perkins, who got off along the way to visit his family.

We had another 'bit of a do' in the Jones's house in Goodwood street after an evening where much ale had already been supped in the Brittania pub opposite, celebrating our nuptials.

It was a very boisterous affair, with every surface overflowing with drinks and food and with the dancing going on into the early hours.

On our return, the Central Hotel let us move into a room in their staff house in Golf Terrace as Pat was also working at the Central as a waiter in the restaurant at the time. Winter set in, the staff house was freezing and unwelcoming and with only the one bathroom and toilet, the cleanliness of the other staff occupants in the house left a lot to be desired.

I'd continually scrub the bathroom, but the toilet was stained, the bath had a constant tide mark, and everything just felt grimy. The chef in the Central at the time was Larry, a happy go lucky chap whose straggly and greasy hair I begrudgingly agreed to cut every so often. Just so that he'd slip me a nice couple of steaks from the Central's larder now and again or a lamb chop or two for me to cook in the miniscule kitchen in the staff house, for our Sunday roast.

Once Christmas was over, I couldn't take it anymore and badgered Mum and Dad to let us move into Treninnick Tavern, as the bedrooms were no longer in use for guests and I was desperate to get out of Golf Terrace, if only to feel clean again.

Dad needed help in the bar by then, so Pat left the Central and started working at the Tavern as a full-time barman and we moved into the large front bedroom above the restaurant bar in the Spring of 1972.

The night of the bust-up, I had just finished a long shift at the Central, walked all the way home and was sitting on a stool at the end of the restaurant bar, chatting to Pat and enjoying a bit of relaxation. It was 10 o'clock.

'Clear those tables,' Mum ordered me, no doubt annoyed I was sitting doing nothing.

'Mum, I've only just finished, I'm shattered.'

Well, if you're living in this house, then you have to muck in,' she added.

'She's only just finished her shift,' Pat said defensively.

'Well you wanted to live here, and if you don't like it you know what you can do.'

And so, it started. The arguing. With tempers frayed in the middle of a busy Summer Season, on and on, out into the hallway, up the stairs to our room, saying or rather shouting all those things they'd both been desperate to say to each other for so long. Escalating out of control, ending up with a slanging match between the two of them.

With me in floods of tears, having packed a bag, we walked out of the Pub that night. It was 10.30 p.m.

Frank and Kath, our friends lived in a cottage at the back of the Pub, so we knocked on their door. We had nowhere else to go.

The next morning after a fitful night's sleep, I was due to have an interview for the position of manageress of the new Dorothy Perkins store due to open on Bank street in Newquay. The interviews were to be held up at the Headland Hotel. I wanted a change and a new challenge, but little did I feel like going.

Nevertheless, I made the long walk from Treninnick up to the Headland, not having much hope of getting anywhere.

A couple of days later, I had no choice but to go back home to collect some more things, with Dad trying to calm the waters yet again. But too many things had been said between Mum and Pat to even contemplate getting them together in the same room, let alone speaking again.

We only stayed a couple of nights with Frank and Kath, until Pat found us a room to rent in a house on the Mayfield estate. I was still in the Central, but he was now out of a job, so went back to the Marina Hotel as a waiter.

That room was a nightmare. The house belonged to a divorced young woman who loved to have music on late at night when she brought her boyfriend back. Our room had two single beds and a wardrobe and that was about it. I cried every night.

As soon as we could, once the peak of the season was over, we rented a cottage on Chapel Hill, just behind the Central, which had two bedrooms, a lovely open fireplace and large kitchen. It was heaven. At least for a few months.

To my surprise, I had been shortlisted for the Dorothy Perkins job and the final interview between the last two candidates was to be in London. I'd been up front with the Shortland's in the Central about the job, so they let me have the time off.

I knew the other girl up for the position and we sat near one another on the train and although I wasn't in the right state of mind, gave it my best shot. But when I saw that she had taken a change of clothes with her which she changed into just before we reached London, so she looked smart and fresh, I knew it was game over. I had the same crimplene dress on that I'd worn to the first interview.

I settled back into the Central and we had lovely log fires in the cottage. Despite it being mid-Winter, Pat's Dad and his youngest brother Paul were due to come and stay with us for a week from Liverpool. We'd given them instructions where to change trains to get to Newquay station and we'd lit a lovely big fire, which was roaring away up the chimney and had dinner ready in the oven. They were due any minute.

Then there was a knock on the cottage door.

'We've just had a phone call from Pat's Dad,' said Mrs. Shortland from the Central. *'They got off at Par by mistake and there are no more trains tonight,'*

After thanking her and dousing the fire best we could, we set off in the car for Par, not having a clue how to get there and if that weren't bad enough, it was foggy.

I'm sure we went around one roundabout the wrong way, before we eventually arrived and found his Dad, sitting on a bench on the platform, nonchalantly puffing away on his pipe. Wearing a hat with corks dangling from it, like the Aussies wear, with not a care in the world. Pat called him all the names under the sun.

His Dad, Chic, was a one off. If anything was going to happen, it was going to happen to him!

We knew we'd have to get out of the cottage as soon as the holiday season kicked off again and knowing we didn't have a permanent place to live, we made the decision to leave Newquay for pastures new. Pat hadn't seen or spoken to my Mum and Dad since the bust up and I made one last strained visit to the Pub, before we left. Mum gave me a writing case with a Basildon Bond pad inside. making me promise to write to her, wherever we ended up.

With that, in the Spring of 1973, we packed up all our belongings we had in the cottage into a couple of suitcases and multitude of carrier bags, walked to the bus station and caught the early bus to the train station. We were on our way to London.

I'd been desperate to leave Cornwall for a long while, thinking there was no future for us there.

I was eager to see other places and to seek out new opportunities. Sound familiar? My parents had left London for Cornwall all those years before and here was I doing the exact opposite and leaving Cornwall for London.

I knew we had to get away from the toxic situation between Pat and my Mum and the only way to do that was to leave and put some distance between the two of them.

I think Mum was shocked when I chose Pat over her, but she shouldn't have expected anything less. I could be as stubborn as she and finally, long overdue, I was making my own way in life and making my own decisions.

As we waved goodbye to Newquay, not knowing what the future would hold and if or when we'd ever be back, I was excited.

Oh my, what *was* I thinking!

Epilogue
Into the Frying Pan

George, Pat's mate was waiting for us at Paddington station when we arrived off the train from Newquay. He'd arranged jobs for us at The Essex Centre hotel in Basildon, where he was working.

The interviews were merely a formality, so we started there in Spring 1973, Pat as waiter and me as receptionist. It was helpful to have jobs to walk straight into, but we didn't intend being there long. We had other plans.

Before we'd left Cornwall, we'd applied to Watney's Brewery in London to train as Pub Managers. After we'd had the interview in their offices in Whitechapel in the East end of London, we stopped off for a drink in the infamous Blind Beggar pub, which was just around the corner. Notorious as being where Ronnie Kray murdered George Cornell.

We were accepted by Watney's and that Summer, left Basildon and headed off to Tamworth in Surrey, to start their intensive training programme. This included training in Pubs all over London. Being relief managers at first, moving around all over the city, covering for established Pub managers, while they took their holidays.

So, one minute we could be in a busy disco pub in downtown Wimbledon, where the constant swearing turned the air blue and the floor, squelchy and sodden with Guinness. Then we'd pack our bags and go to Esher in Surrey, where the clientele rode horses, drank Pimms and air-kissed for England.

At the end of two weeks at one Pub, we'd be given instructions as to where to turn up to next. Occasionally with a couple of days off in-between. We never knew what we'd be walking into. Our lives and belongings stashed in the old banger we'd bought in Basildon, with nowhere to call home.

We'd thought hotel work was hard enough, with its split shifts, low pay, seasonal work and hard to please guests.

But that was a doddle compared to the punishing hours, copious responsibilities, crazy demented characters that frequented some of the less than reputable establishments, abusive drunks, and sheer turmoil of being Pub managers 24 x 7.

For the next few years, in London, that's exactly what we did, training in and then managing some of the busiest pubs around the Capital and beyond.

My naivety had waned somewhat, thanks to the education I'd received working in the hotels, but my shyness still bubbled up from time to time. But playing the part of a Pub landlady, soon gave me new-found confidence. I was in control, I was the boss, or at least one of them. It was me employing staff, giving orders, telling drunks to get out.

We hardly had time to give Newquay a second thought.

That is, until my Mum and Dad suddenly walked into the Pub we were managing, in Hersham in Surrey, one day. Unexpected. Without warning.

I'd written, but I hadn't spoken to them since leaving Newquay

Pat hadn't spoken to them since 'The Bust up', eighteen months previous.

Uh-oh!

Nowhere to run to, this time!

Glossary & Info

The Minerva hotel still sits in an enviable position overlooking the Killacourt. It has been fully refurbished and modernized and now every room has en-suite, colour TV and drinks station.

The Bristol Hotel is still one of the prestigious hotels in Newquay. Although now part of the Best Western chain, Howard Young is the managing director. Fourth generation of the Young family. All the 74 comfortable rooms are now en-suite.

The Central Hotel although still a popular destination has changed dramatically internally. No longer a hotel, it is now called **The Central Inn** offering a terrace to watch the world go by, whilst enjoying food and drink in the centre of town.

Treninnick Tavern is still a popular venue but is now called **The Tavern Inn.** The layout has changed inside, with another extension added providing additional space for functions. With live music, games room and an appetizing menu, it offers facilities for great family get togethers.

Huer's Hut. Perched on the cliff top high above the harbour the building is thought to date back to the 14th century when it was used as a lookout by a huer. The huer's job was to watch for the tell-tale signs of pilchard shoals and then alert the townsfolk to their arrival.

White Sails, Holywell Bay was knocked down, I believe in the 1980's and there are now five or six properties on the site.

Cornish v Cockney

'Aright, my 'ansum?'	How are you?
'Watcha cock	Hello
'Brahms and Liszt,'.	Pi**ed (Inebriated)
Awright'n aree?	Are you alright?
'Giss on	Are you pulling my leg
' Big Smoke'	London
'Proper job. Bleddy 'ansum	Absolutely fantastic
'Apples and Pears'	Stairs
'Bob Hope'	Soap
'Dreckly	Soon, but don't hold your breath.
'Kent be doing'	I can't have that

MAP OF NEWQUAY

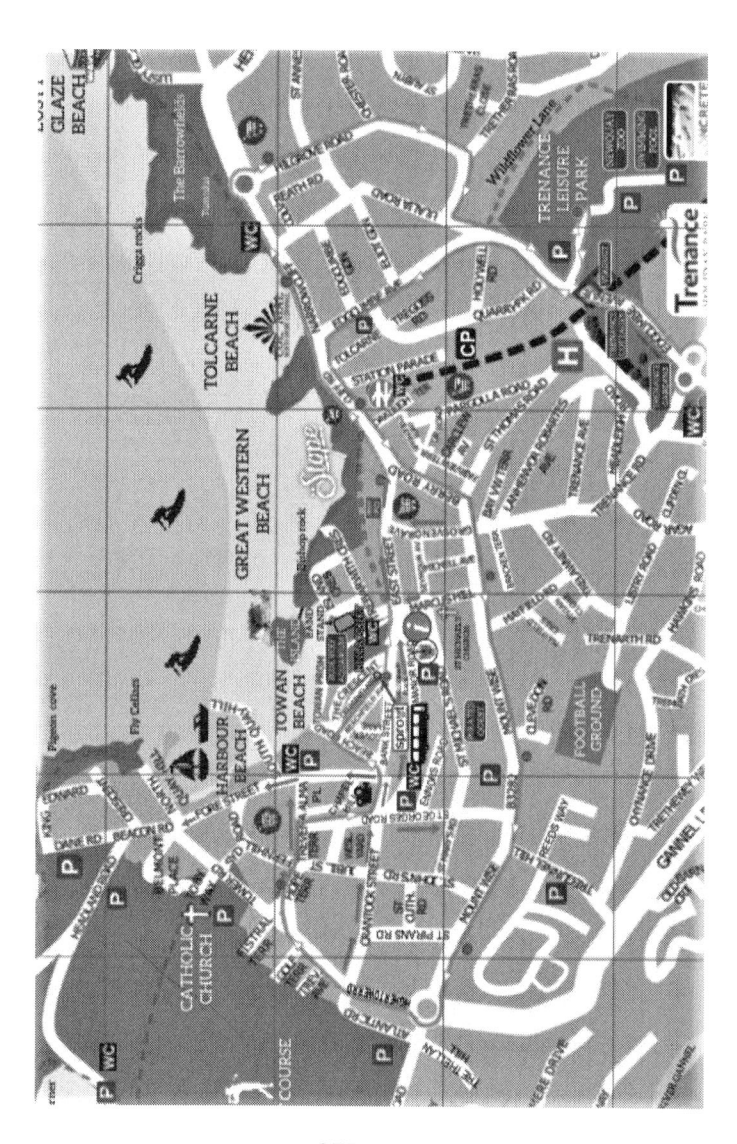

List of Newquay hotels and owners

This is only a snapshot and a fraction of the many hotels in Newquay in the 1960's and these owners didn't necessarily own these hotels at the same time.

Some hotels constantly changed hands from season to season, while others remained in the same family for years.

Hotels	Owners
Atlantic	Pascoe/ Cobley
Riviera	David Nixon
Trebarwith	Tarrant/Knight
Kilbirnie	Barlow
Great Western	Hooper
Glendorgal	Tangye
Edgcumbe	Armstrong
St.Brannocks	Price/Stephens
Victoria	Taylor/Boyden
Bella Vista	Slater
Carnmarth	Hadfield
Windsor	Start
Beresford	Edwards
Kontiki	Cobley
Tremont	Andersons
Cumberland	Faulkner
Trelawney	Ridgement
Falstaff	Taylor

Hotels	Owners
Fistral Bay	Pickles
La Felicia	Ashby
Trenance	Morrell
Beachview	Bedfords
St.Brannocks	Stephens
Trevone	Chegwins
Bredon Court	Carltons
Beachcroft	Briggs, then Price
Tolcarne	Edwards
Rocklands	Brock
Borna	Kippax
Minto	Leverton
Links	Naylor
St.Rumons	Christophilus
Beaconsfield	Carr
Cavendish	Bailey
Grantham Astor	O'Shea
Bewdley	Bedford
Water's Edge	Robinson

Newquay shops

The following pages show some of the shops around in 1967. These are from lists I obtained from an extremely helpful Sheila Harper in the Newquay heritage museum, a few years ago.

It isn't every shop on every street, but it does give a flavour of the shops around at the time, for those with a challenged memory like mine!

<u>East Street</u>	<u>East Street</u>	<u>Fore St</u>
Bus Station	Joan Kay	Jenkin
Book shop	Newquay Motors	Banfield
Gill's Fish shop	Killacourt café	Stephens Cafe
Smugglers cave	Foster Trinimans	Co-op
Mayfair cleaners	Hawkeys tours	Biscombes
		Ministry of
Island stores	Foster Trinimans	Labour
Cottage	Rif Café	Morris
Wimpy Bar	Cornish stone	Atkinson
Radio Rentals	A.E.Jenkin	Wood
Gay Gannet	International	Cadoc Café
Shrimptons	Wesley Chapel	Bellingham
Rawles fish shop	Dentists	Surf Centre
Penunda Café	Bayley studios	Engravers
Beresford motors	Saunders shoes	Cottage café
Avis	Macari's	Mole & Son
		Harbour fruit
Varnalls opticians	Newquay dairy	stores
Scandia	Radfords	Ice cream parlour
Refrigeration Ltd	Wool shop	48 Café
W.V Edwards	Hunkins	Hicks
Hotel (site of new	Huxtable	Marsham Tyres
Post Office)	John Julians	Shirley cottage
Police station	Electrical services	Hawkeys Tours
Smugglers Chest	Hoi Gan chinese	Fruit Basket
Hotel Victoria	Beau Monde	

Central Square	Cliff Road	Bank St
T.Pearce	Michell	R.E.Pearce
Central Sports	Cliff Stores	Wetherall
Lloyds Bank	Leslie hair	Applegates
Walter Williams	Malabu	Midland Bank
R.Coles Ltd	D.Ashwell	Post Office
Quests	Gas showroom	Timothy Whites
Millbay Laundry	Sussex Grill	Walter Hicks
Maynards	Flinn	Oyster Bar
Central Meat	H.Brown	Lennards
Whitehouse	Newquay motors	Cornish Silk
Mathews Dairy	Seaspray	W.H.Smith
		Hawke & Thomas
Mathews Café	Varley	Devenish brewery
	Surfriders	Paul Drake
	Quoit dairy	Menzies
	Hawkeys tours	Hoopers Café
	Lloyds Bank	Boots
	Betting office	Radio Rental
	Cabaret club	Watch & Clock
	Midland bank	Gay Gowns
	Edgcumbe stores	Lawleys
		Westminster Bank
		Land, Sea & Air

Author Bio

Hi there,

Although I've always dabbled in writing, I didn't take it seriously until early retirement in 2006. I took several writing courses and am currently a member of Formby Writers on Merseyside, who are a constant source of inspiration, support, and motivation.

Writing about real life is my passion. Doing the research and crafting an article is so enjoyable. But I also love to write humorous poems, competition slogans as well as filler or shorter pieces. To date I have had over fifty pieces of my writing published or won writing competitions in a wide variety of places, including well known magazines and newspapers as well as online. This is my first book.

I was extremely lucky to grow up in Cornwall and although I have lived on Merseyside for over 40 years, I consider Newquay, to still be my home.

Denise Jones

Printed in Great Britain
by Amazon